SURVIVING the COMING TAX DISASTER

SURVIVING the COMING TAX DISASTER

Why Taxes Are Going Up,

How the IRS Will Be Getting

More Aggressive, and *What* You Can

Do to Preserve Your Assets

RONI DEUTCH

BENBELLA

BENBELLA BOOKS, INC.

Dallas, TX

BenBella Books, Inc.
10300 N. Central Expressway, Suite 400
Dallas, TX 75231
www.benbellabooks.com
Send feedback to feedback@benbellabooks.com

Printed in the United States of America
10 9 8 7 6 5 4 3 2 1

Library of Congress Cataloging-in-Publication Data is available for this title.
ISBN: 978-1-935618-07-2

Copyediting by Erin Kelley
Proofreading by Greg Teague and Erica Lovett
Cover design by Faceout Studio
Text design and composition by PerfecType, Nashville, TN
Charts and graphs by Sean Bellows
Printed by Bang Printing

Distributed by Perseus Distribution
perseusdistribution.com

To place orders through Perseus Distribution:
Tel: 800-343-4499
Fax: 800-351-5073
E-mail: orderentry@perseusbooks.com

Significant discounts for bulk sales are available. Please contact Glenn Yeffeth at glenn@benbellabooks.com or (214) 750-3628.

Dedication

I dedicate this book to my beautiful niece, Jamie Ross. I love you, sweetheart, and feel extremely blessed to be your Aunt, Mentor, and Friend. Thank you for spoiling me with your gorgeous smile, your soulful eyes, and your tender heart. I believe in everything you are and everything you are going to be. As our dear friend Mary Poppins would say, "Reach for Heaven and the stars will be thrown in." You are my Heaven, my Rock Star, my Little Charlie. Let's load the car and go to 7-11…we can even bring your brothers! Here's to being an Aunt, the greatest joy and privilege in the world!!

Table of Contents

Introduction

This old saying is often quoted as both a proverb and a curse. I think the last few years prove just how frightening "interesting times" can be.

Rampant unemployment. A feeble stock market. Housing values that have gone so far south that penguins have been sighted nibbling on foreclosure signs.

That's how bad things are.

How do we get out of this rut? Well, that's up for debate. Since 2008, our government has spent almost $2 trillion in bailout money. It appears the federal government has decided bailouts are the way to go. But that money will not come out of thin air. So where will Washington get all this cash? There are two ways:

1. By selling U.S. bonds in the public fixed income market, primarily to overseas institutional investors, like China and India.
2. By extracting more money from the greatest tax base in the entire world—the U.S. taxpayer.

With record-breaking deficits and no solution in sight, fewer investors are willing to buy U.S. bonds, which means that the government is turning toward the second option: squeezing every penny out of every taxpayer it can.

You see, Uncle Sam has no intention of being stuck with the tab—not with 156 million chickens to pluck. And make no mistake, if you're behind on your taxes, no matter how few feathers you have left, the IRS is coming after you.

Just when most Americans are down on their luck and hurting financially, the IRS is gearing up for its biggest collection campaign ever. Don't let the "kinder, gentler" public relations campaign fool you. The IRS exists to collect money from people just like you, regardless of your ability to pay. That's the real tragedy.

In the best of times, 20 percent of U.S. taxpayers fall behind on their taxes. And these are far from the best of times, meaning more people than ever are being sucked into the IRS collection machine.

The reasons are common enough. A job loss, an injury or illness, foreclosure, divorce, death of a family member, a small business going under in the brutal economy—any one of these unforeseen catastrophes can push even the most frugal person or family over the edge and into despair.

Apparently, all the turmoil is pushing the IRS over the edge, too. With tax revenues struggling to keep up with government spending, the IRS is looking for cash. And the danger is that the full weight of the IRS monolith may land on *you* when you are least able to take it. Between increasingly aggressive collection efforts, higher taxes across the board, brand new taxes popping up, and more audits than ever, the IRS will do everything within its power to wring every penny from each of us.

In case after case, I have seen firsthand that Uncle Sam will pull no punches in taking advantage of a taxpayer who might be uninformed about U.S. tax laws or IRS audit and collection procedures. It's been my stance that taxpayers not only need but deserve to be protected from IRS abuse and intimidation. This is why I've committed my adult life to guarding people against the calamity of owing the IRS. Believe me, *calamity* isn't too strong a word. If you get behind in your payments to the IRS, no matter what the reason, the consequences are harsh.

If you fall behind on your taxes, the IRS can do a lot to destroy your finances, including:

- **Wage Garnishments**
  A wage garnishment is exactly what it sounds like—the IRS can capture back taxes by raiding your paycheck and taking what it deems necessary. Depending upon your financial situation, the IRS can end up taking the entire thing!
- **Tax Levies**
  A tax levy is a legal seizure of your property to satisfy a tax debt. Yes, the IRS can come take the cash right out of your savings or checking account. And that is without regard to any outstanding checks you may have written for your home, car, utilities, or business.
- **Tax Liens**
  A tax lien works like a lock on your home and any other personal property you own, meaning you can't sell the property without the IRS laying claim to the proceeds. A tax lien can kill your home's value in addition to wreaking havoc on your credit rating!

- **Mounting Interest and Penalties**

  When the IRS comes collecting an unpaid debt, it wants it all, including the additional penalties it has added and the daily accruing interest. These extra fees can add 5 percent of your total debt per month and, if your tax return is late and unpaid, up to 100 percent!

- **Ruined Credit**

  Of all the financial penalties inflicted on late payers, a tax lien can do the most damage. Why? Because a tax lien actually shows up on your credit report, highlighting you as a deadbeat in the eyes of the world. If a tax lien shows up on your credit report, it can take up to seven years to make it vanish.

This is to say nothing about the *emotional* anxiety that the IRS can bring to the table in a collection scenario. The agency is relentless, remorseless, and without conscience.

And yet, there are even *more* ways it collects from you. As you will see in chapters 4 through 8, the IRS is especially vicious when you are already down for the count. Specifically, the IRS will come after you when you lose your home, lose your job, close your business, suffer a personal crisis, or make adjustments to your retirement plan. Yes, as I have said, the IRS has shown no signs of humility in its passion for collection.

Please don't misunderstand me. I'm a fervent believer in paying our taxes on time, and paying what we owe. As the old saying goes, taxes are the price we pay for a civilized, orderly republic.

But I've been in the trenches too long to look at the IRS as anything other than an unscrupulous, vengeful bully, no better than a schoolyard tough guy beating up little kids who don't cough up their lunch money.

Sure, I hear stories about how our elected officials are going to enact laws that will make the IRS a kinder, gentler federal agency.

But I've come to think of our political leaders as being more of the problem than the solution when it comes to protecting taxpayers.

That's why I got a big kick out of a story in 2009 when our U.S. Treasury Secretary and a powerful New York congressman were busted for back tax liabilities. I bet many people don't realize that both politicians' cases were settled without them having to pay penalties on their outstanding taxes—a perk that the average American would be hard-pressed to get.

At least one congressman gets it. Rep. John Carter (R-TX) introduced a bill to Congress stating that all U.S. taxpayers would enjoy the same immunity from IRS penalties and interest as Rep. Charles Rangel (D-NY) and Treasury Secretary Timothy Geithner—the beneficiaries of the IRS's benevolent treatment. "We must show the American people that Congress is following the same law and the same legal process as we expect them to follow," Carter said in front of Congress.

Under the proposed "Rangel Rule Act of 2009" (which didn't stand a chance of passing), any taxpayer who wrote "Rangel Rule" on his or her return when paying back taxes would be immune from penalties and interest. "If we don't hold our highest elected officials to the same standards as regular working folks, we owe it to our constituents to change those standards so everyone is abiding by the same law," Carter added. He also said that the change in tax law would provide good economic stimulus benefits, "as it would free many taxpayers from massive debts to the IRS, restoring those funds to the free market to help create jobs."

Ha! My kind of guy.

But until we see some commonsense legislation from our leaders in Washington, we're stuck with the tax system we've got. And believe me, it's a lousy one, where the deck is stacked against the average Joe and Jane.

That's why it's time to take back our country from the grip of the IRS. In this book, I'm going to explain how the federal government is using the ongoing financial crisis to take more money out of the hides of taxpayers. I will explain how the IRS will try to collect more revenue, and what steps you can take to stop the IRS in its tracks. No matter if you have lost your home, your job, your business, or even your health, I'm going to teach you how to fight back. I'll show you how you can get your own "tax bailout" if you know the right moves.

Now, I want you to be well-informed about our current economic situation—how we got here and what you can to do protect yourself. So, in this book I will lay out the cold hard facts. In chapters 1 through 3, you will get a big dose of how we, as a nation, got into this economic mess and why the IRS will be looking to all taxpayers to bail it out of its financial pit.

Chapters 4 through 6 will guide you through the effects of our current economic state; I'll discuss foreclosures, unemployment, and bankruptcy, to name a few. In the final chapters, you will be given specific tools to assist you in protecting your assets against the pending IRS storm.

That's the goal of this book—it's a much-needed lifeline for Americans laid low by the brutal economic climate who, through the loss of job, illness, or foreclosure (among other financial hardships), struggle to pay their taxes.

So let's climb aboard and ride the wave together. When it comes to beating the IRS at the tax game, I like to say, "I'm in it to win it."

Join me and I'll show you how you, too, can win.

—Roni Deutch

How Bad Is It?

America is moving forward and gaining strength. We have been tested, and we have proven ourselves to be a tough, resilient, and resourceful nation.

—BILL FRIST

Amerca has a long history of turning lemons into lemonade. Back in the late 1970s, the United States was hit by a massive recession. Nightclub owners couldn't afford to pay bands enough to keep the doors open every night. Instead, they bought sound systems and launched disco as the biggest musical movement of the decade.

Resiliency is a great characteristic for a nation, and one that we have in abundance here in the United States. Trust me; we're going to need resiliency in the years ahead, as we slowly escape the clutches of the worst economy since the Great Depression.

I'm not saying we're in another Great Depression, but there's no doubt about it—times are tough, so we have to be tough, too.

So, how exactly did we get here?

Call it a perfect storm of economic destruction—a toxic maelstrom of bad banking decisions, worse government decisions, and the natural entitlement mentality of way too many people who used credit to live way beyond their means. Let's take a look at some of the specific elements of the perfect storm:

- Massive consumer debt. As of January 2010, government figures show that U.S. revolving consumer debt, made up almost entirely of credit card debt, was about $864 billion. In the fourth quarter of 2008, 13.9 percent of consumer disposable income went to service this debt.

- Increase of the U.S. government debt by at least $2 trillion in 2009. By December of 2009, the U.S. government debt was 86.3 percent of the Gross Domestic Product (GDP). Let me put this into context for you: before the Great Depression in 1929, the U.S. government debt was only 15 percent of GDP.

- A complete mispricing of money, along with some flashy financial innovations, led to the housing boom and allowed buyers to purchase homes without down payments and existing homeowners to refinance mortgages.

- Add to the mix a consumption boom, unmatched, at least here in the United States, by an equal amount of industrial production and capital spending increases.

- Expansion of the U.S. deficit and the current account deficit to $115.6 billion from $102.3 billion in third quarter 2009, and a GDP increase to 3.2 percent from 2.9 percent.

A Downward Spiral

With those ingredients in place, it took only a few short years to reach economic destruction. We watched in dismay as our financial structures collapsed around the modern world. When the economy crashes this far, the dominoes that inevitably fall are sequoia-sized.

For instance, cash-strapped banks are calling in all their outstanding loans to stay afloat. In extreme cases, homeowners are forced to pay their entire outstanding mortgage over a few short months! The same story is happening with credit card companies—some are demanding full and immediate payment from card carriers, most of whom aren't able to pay off their debt in a single payment. American Express even offered their less stable customers $300 to *close* their credit card accounts.

When customers don't pay, credit card companies accelerate the death spiral by hiking interest rates and late payment penalties, even for customers in good standing, in order to bring in additional revenue to offset losses from bad business decisions. My short version: any Americans who have undertaken significant debt stand to lose everything they own.

Ironically, although consumer debts are crippling the average American, our politicians are borrowing and spending at a rate that would trigger heartburn in a used car salesman. Take our federal debt: our $12.5 trillion national debt threatens our ability to issue bonds, borrow money, and create the kind of jobs the United States needs to compete on a global basis.

U.S. Government (Federal) Total Receipts

Estimated receipts for fiscal year 2010 are $2.381 trillion (estimated decrease of 11 percent from 2009).

- $1.061 trillion—Individual income tax
- $940 billion—Social Security and other payroll taxes
- $222 billion—Corporate income tax
- $77 billion—Excise taxes
- $23 billion—Customs duties
- $20 billion—Estate and gift taxes
- $16 billion—Other

According to news reports, the president's budget for 2010 totaled $3.8 trillion. This budget request is broken down by the following expenditures (percentages in parentheses indicate percentage of change compared to 2009):

Mandatory spending: $2.184 trillion (+15.6 percent)*

- $695 billion—Social Security
- $453 billion—Medicare
- $290 billion—Medicaid and the State Children's Health Insurance Program (SCHIP)
- $571 billion—Unemployment/Welfare/Other mandatory spending
- $164 billion—Interest on National Debt

Discretionary spending: $1.39 trillion (+13.1 percent)

- $663.7 billion—United States Department of Defense
- $145.2 billion—Global War on Terror
- $78.7 billion—United States Department of Health and Human Services
- $46.7 billion—United States Department of Education
- $52.5 billion—United States Department of Veterans Affairs
- $47.5 billion—United States Department of Housing and Urban Development
- $51.7 billion—State and Other International Programs
- $42.7 billion—United States Department of Homeland Security
- $26.3 billion—United States Department of Energy
- $26.0 billion—United States Department of Agriculture
- $23.9 billion—United States Department of Justice
- $18.7 billion—National Aeronautics and Space Administration
- $13.3 billion—United States Department of the Treasury

> ## Discretionary spending: $1.39 trillion (continued)
>
> - $72.5 billion—United States Department of Transportation
> - $12.0 billion—United States Department of the Interior
> - $13.3 billion—United States Department of Labor
> - $9.7 billion—Social Security Administration
> - $10.5 billion—United States Environmental Protection Agency
> - $7.0 billion—National Science Foundation
> - $6.3 billion—Judicial branch (United States federal courts)
> - $4.7 billion—Legislative branch (United States Congress)
> - $5.1 billion—United States Army Corps of Engineers
> - $0.4 billion—Executive Office of the President
> - $0.7 billion—Small Business Administration
> - $7.2 billion—Other agencies
> - $39.0 billion (2008*)—Other Off-budget Discretionary Spending
>
> *Note: The Iraq War and the War in Afghanistan are not part of the defense budget; they are appropriations.*
> *Source:* Budget of the United States Government: Fiscal year 2010

Adding more fuel to the fire, our baby boomer generation continues to collect Medicare, Medicaid, and Social Security in stipends that average more than $1.69 billion per day.

Other factors are also contributing to this bleak situation:

- A devalued dollar, which is fueling the current run-up in energy and health care prices.
- A lack of domestic savings on the part of Americans and the erosion of the U.S. industrial base.
- The recently passed health care reform law, which carries a hefty price tag over the next nineteen years. Economic experts at the Health and Human Services Department issued a report analyzing the actual cost of the health care overhaul. The report found that the overhaul will increase national

health care spending by $311 billion from 2010–2019, or nine-tenths of one percent. To put that in perspective, total health care spending during the decade is estimated to surpass $35 trillion.

- Import trade imbalances that could cost U.S. businesses and consumers tens of billions of dollars.

I've got to tell you, these trends erode the economic landscape, creating an environment that will lead to a significantly lower standard of living for debt-ravaged Americans and a wobbly stock market that could sink even lower than the 50 percent decline in value we've seen since the market high of October 2007.

I'm all for hope and change and I, too, want our government to succeed. But I want to see our government be smart about it. Many of the tactics the government enacted at the beginning of the new administration, including the $787 billion, 1,074-page stimulus bill, may ultimately intensify the problem, making economic recovery even more elusive. This crash could potentially lead to extreme financial, political, and social unrest.

Other gloomy realities are still playing out:

- A stock market crash as bad as that of the Great Depression could trigger a trading shutdown, losing 50 percent on the first massive plunge and, within two years, sliding to less than 5,000 points on the Dow. It's not so far-fetched.
- Mutual fund investors will be trapped and ultimately panic as they try to pull money out of their funds, leading to further investor flight from the $7 trillion mutual fund market—a market that, within a few years, could lose well over half its value.
- Pension plans are being devastated and retirees will be getting far less than they expected, a trend that's already occurring at a number of U.S. companies.

- Average American asset values could plunge by 80 percent. With stock market losses in the trillions, mutual funds battered, and job security non-existent, Americans have no wiggle room to cope with this type of economic disaster.

- The dollar could lose up to 50 percent of its value if we just keep borrowing and spending and printing more money. That leads to inflation and to a weaker U.S. currency. That picture won't improve if talks about a China-and-Russia-backed new world currency become a reality.

- The Federal Reserve is fast becoming the most scrutinized institution in America as it struggles to right the country's economic ship. Its hand forced by the specter of rising inflation, the Fed will eventually hike interest rates dramatically to prop up the dollar and keep inflation at bay, potentially pricing American consumers out of the real estate market and the auto market and stopping them from borrowing to pay off their accumulating debts.

- Real estate could fall even further, up to 50 percent of peak values. Homeowners are facing record foreclosures and mortgage lenders are going belly-up.

- The financial health of the Social Security system has eroded more sharply in 2009 than at any time since the mid-1990s. The trust fund that pays for hospital care under Medicare is now predicted to run out of money in 2017, two years earlier than was forecasted in 2009.

- As of November 30, 2009, there were 115,000 U.S. troops in Iraq; when our soldiers come home, they will find themselves returning to a damaged economy that will not be able to provide ample veterans' benefits, employment, health care coverage, and education.

- All government guarantees, insurance, and retirement programs will be jeopardized.

The United States is the world's biggest debtor nation, recklessly printing money to sustain the illusion of prosperity; we've been doing this for years. As I mentioned, our national debt liability in 2009 was $12 trillion and rising—the government spending hikes under President Obama will only worsen that deficit.

For decades, Americans have been told by the government, by Wall Street, and by mass media that the economy is just fine even as disaster grows below the surface. Consider these points:

The Deficit

A slew of government and private analysts, plus the actual Government Accountability Office (GAO), Office of Management and Budget (OMB), and the Treasury Department, have warned that debt levels will increase dramatically relative to historical levels if entitlement programs are not reformed. For example, projected expenditures for Medicare and Social Security programs exceed tax revenues by more than $40 trillion over the next seventy-five years. Mandatory expenditures are projected to exceed federal tax revenues sometime between 2030 and 2040 if reforms are not undertaken. The severity of the measures necessary to address this challenge increases the longer such changes are delayed. These organizations have stated that the government's current fiscal path is "unsustainable."

The huge U.S. budget deficit is the single biggest driver of U.S. economic woes. To meet liabilities, Americans will see dramatic changes in the financial landscape—changes that could well put a majority of Americans in financial hardship—at a time when the federal government will come looking for more money, with its henchmen from the IRS acting as collection agents.

For a good look at how the government spends so much of our money, check out this graph:

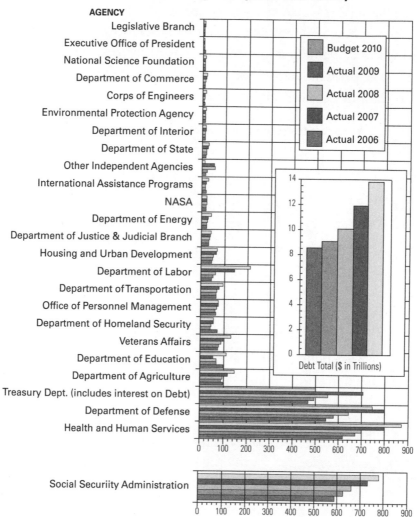

How Congress Spends Your Money

AGENCY

Legislative Branch
Executive Office of President
National Science Foundation
Department of Commerce
Corps of Engineers
Environmental Protection Agency
Department of Interior
Department of State
Other Independent Agencies
International Assistance Programs
NASA
Department of Energy
Department of Justice & Judicial Branch
Housing and Urban Development
Department of Labor
Department of Transportation
Office of Personnel Management
Department of Homeland Security
Veterans Affairs
Department of Education
Department of Agriculture
Treasury Dept. (includes interest on Debt)
Department of Defense
Health and Human Services

Budget 2010
Actual 2009
Actual 2008
Actual 2007
Actual 2006

Debt Total ($ in Trillions)

Social Securiity Administration

The Dollar

How dire is the dollar situation these days? I'll put it this way: If
someone offered U.S. investors a bond that pays zero interest, has
zero collateral, lost 25 percent of its value in the last three years, and
has dropped by 90 percent in the last sixty-one years, would investors be interested?

I don't think so. But that's basically the deal with the U.S. dollar these days. I'd say we're in a precarious position.

To see how government spending has devalued the U.S. currency and what that has meant to Americans financially, examine the following two graphs. One graph depicts the rate of government spending; the other shows the decline of U.S. household wealth. It's a scary correlation.

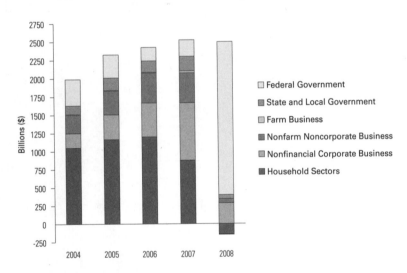

Total Net Borrowing and Lending in Credit Markets

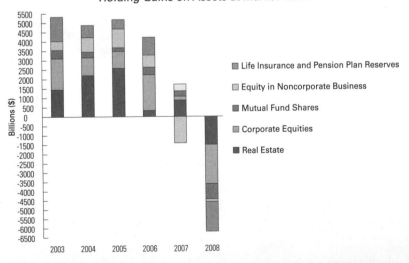

Change in Net Worth of Households and Nonprofit Organizations
Holding Gains on Assets at Market Value

The Stock Market

U.S. equities remain substantially overvalued, and the major U.S. stock indexes are in the early stages of long-term bear markets.

In fact, economic policy decisions by the U.S. Federal Reserve have greased the skids for the stock market's demise, primarily by flooding the world with dollars and credit. Also, a climate of higher taxes will crimp company profits and reduce stock value. It's pretty simple: lower profits mean lower stock prices. Just like Americans, foreign investors have watched their stock market wealth disappear. Overseas, American investments are becoming less and less attractive, and foreigner investors may soon abandon the dollar altogether.

Bonds

Meanwhile, a cash flood is also washing overseas. Foreigners now hold trillions in U.S. investments, yet we keep going back to these investors with hat in hand, asking them to invest and buy even more of our Treasury bonds, at interest rates that our grandchildren will be paying for. That is a vicious cycle.

Real Estate

There's no great trick to understanding the current status of the U.S. real estate market. If it looks like a bubble, walks like a bubble, and quacks like a bubble, it's a bubble.

The combination of artificially low interest rates; foreign central bank intervention; an irresponsible Fed; excessive credit availability; the proliferation of low- or no-down-payment, adjustable rate, interest only, negative amortization mortgages; a can't-lose attitude among speculators, validated by ever-rising "comps"; the complete abandonment of lending standards; widespread corruption in the appraisal industry; and rampant fraud among sub-prime lenders has produced the "mother of all bubbles," a bubble that has already burst. And it's not just real estate speculators and homeowners who are suffering; it's the entire U.S. economy, the banking and financial systems, and anyone with U.S.-dollar-denominated savings.

The U.S. real estate market grew too far, too fast—and now it's in freefall. How bad is it? The median value of a U.S. home in 2000 was $119,600. In 2006, the median value peaked at $221,900; in 2009, it fell to $170,000. Look at the following chart to see how far home prices have fallen.

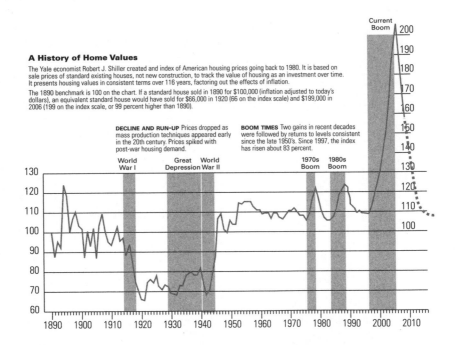

A History of Home Values

The Yale economist Robert J. Shiller created and index of American housing prices going back to 1980. It is based on sale prices of standard existing houses, not new construction, to track the value of housing as an investment over time. It presents housing values in consistent terms over 116 years, factoring out the effects of inflation.

The 1890 benchmark is 100 on the chart. If a standard house sold in 1890 for $100,000 (inflation adjusted to today's dollars), an equivalent standard house would have sold for $66,000 in 1920 (66 on the index scale) and $199,000 in 2006 (199 on the index scale, or 99 percent higher than 1890).

DECLINE AND RUN-UP Prices dropped as mass production techniques appeared early in the 20th century. Prices spiked with post-war housing demand.

BOOM TIMES Two gains in recent decades were followed by returns to levels consistent since the late 1950's. Since 1997, the index has risen about 83 percent.

There is also the worry that the federal government, in cahoots with the Federal Reserve, will re-inflate the housing bubble with its program of buying up mortgage securities. Usually, that's done in the private market. Through the end of 2009, the Federal Reserve had poured $1.25 trillion into "artificially" pumping up the U.S. mortgage market. The question is: What happens when the Fed stops buying those mortgages?

Interest Rates

The U.S. dollar has dropped precipitously in recent years. In response, the Federal Reserve has dropped rates to historic lows to get banks lending money and get consumers and businesses borrowing again. (As I said, this cannot last. When inflation rears its ugly head, as it always does in times of economic strife, the Fed will be forced to raise rates to control the money supply and tamp down inflation.) In an effort to push the collapse off into the future, the dropping of interest rates to near-zero levels created a frenzy of lending, as people rushed out to continue to live beyond their means. With loan interest near 5 percent, those burned in the stock market went out and invested in real estate.

The biggest gains, double-digit in many cases, have been taken out of the real estate market. The Federal Reserve belatedly realized this, beginning the process of hiking interest rates to curb easy credit and rampant speculation in the real estate market.

Higher interest rates are further complicating matters across the U.S. economic landscape. Higher rates result in a rise in the cost of adjustable rate mortgages and other floating rate debt; higher interest rates also crush consumer spending and result in greater shares of household incomes going to debt service.

Consumer Debt (and Bad Economic Calculations)

We consumers have had a hand in this financial mess, too. Data as of February 2010 shows that total U.S. consumer debt (which includes credit card debt and noncredit card debt but not mortgage debt) reached $2.55 trillion at the end of 2007, up from $2.42 trillion at the end of 2006, according to the Federal Reserve.

There is no doubt the U.S. consumer is debt burdened, with the debt-to-disposable-income ratio having increased from 70 percent in the early 1990s to 100 percent in 2000 and to 140 percent in 2009. Worse, not only are debt ratios high and rising, debt-servicing ratios are high and rising, too, having gone from 11 percent in 2000 to almost 15 percent now, as the interest rate on mortgages and consumer debt is resetting at higher levels.

Fortunately, most Americans have started to realize the danger we are in, as savings levels have started to increase for the first time in decades.

To see how badly the ratio between household savings and household debt has gotten, check out this graph:

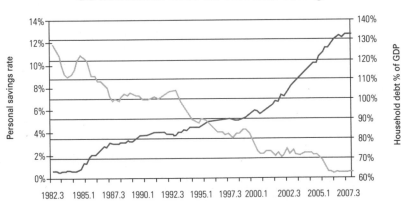

US Household Debt vs. Personal Savings

What does the future hold? It's hard to say for sure, but we're definitely entering a new era in America—a "new normal" where our standard of living is definitely in decline. Given the sequence of events I've laid out here, this is inevitable. Some economists insisted that the United States was "too big to fail," saying that foreign creditors would never tire of loaning America enormous amounts of money at low interest rates. Well, that era is coming to a close.

Going forward, the future looks a lot like the present. As interest rates rise, borrowers are realizing that they have paid way too much for houses and other assets, and committed to interest payments they cannot afford to make and principals they will never be able to repay.

Lenders are also realizing they have recklessly lent money to noncreditworthy borrowers, based on insufficient collateral and pie-in-the-sky assumptions. As credit contracts and asset prices fell, so did consumer spending, along with the consumption-based economy it supports.

Americans who are caught with a substantial amount of debt can expect rising interest rates, causing slow payments, then no payment, resulting in a stampede by banks, creditors, and lenders to get their money back. As more houses are foreclosed on and businesses close their doors, the once-affluent Americans will find themselves in the twenty-first-century version of the soup line, looking for ways to feed and shelter their families.

All of this has caused:

- Net worth of individual households to be turned upside down, with reverse-wealth effects restraining consumption for years to come.
- Millions of people to lose their jobs. Because the majority of American workers depend on the discretionary spending of other Americans, millions more have become unemployed, forcing millions of consumers into bankruptcy.

- Nearly every American to feel some effect of the financial crisis. Especially hard-hit industries are the mortgage and consumer finance, home building, real estate sales, financial services, travel, entertainment, and retailing sectors.

It seems that the U.S. government, including the IRS, is expecting each American to chip in and help bail Big Business and each other out of this mess.

Granted, the information I've laid out here in chapter 1 is probably more suitable to a Stephen King novel than it is to a book on fighting the IRS. But there is always a method to the Tax Lady's madness. I'm laying the groundwork here in chapter 1 for the rest of the book. With all of the debt we've incurred and all the spending we've undertaken, the U.S. government—and our economy—is in a world of hurt.

To finance this spend-a-palooza, the government is going to get even more aggressive about coming after American taxpayers, especially those who are already behind on their payments to the IRS.

You have to be ready when it comes knocking on your door. As you can see, the financial stakes are higher than at perhaps any time in our history. The IRS is not going to be polite about it and is going to do everything it can to collect as much tax money as possible.

The good news? The Tax Lady is on the case.

The "Real" Unemployment Number

Here's a little-known fact: the actual unemployment number is much higher than the government lets on. For example, the 10.2 percent unemployment rate at the end of 2009 would have actually been closer to 18 percent if the government counted part-time workers, freelancers, and other self-employed folks, and those who simply stopped looking for work.

I have my own ideas on how to get out of this mess. I was on FOX Business a while back and presented some concrete solutions to the economic crisis.

"These bailouts are going to cost taxpayers billions of dollars," I told FOX Business viewers. "The government is going to have to raise taxes across the board. Just raising taxes on the wealthy will not be enough to cover these expenses."

During the segment, the show's host asked me what I would do if I were president.

"I truly believe you either reduce spending, borrow money, or you grow trees that produce money," I said. "Currently, 15 to 20 percent of taxpayers cannot pay their bills, so raising taxes on those people will be difficult. We need to think about reducing spending somewhere, and I think the best place to do so is in military and defense spending. The solution to this financial crisis has to be balanced. Reduce spending, and raise taxes just a little."

Right now, I'm not sure that's exactly the direction we're going. If we stray from the path of commonsense, kitchen table economics, then we'll be bogged down for a long time.

And we'll never get the IRS off our backs.

Common Misconceptions about the Wall Street Bailout

Obviously, I have a lot to say about all this government spending we've seen in the past few years. I've even come up with a list of "myths" and "realities" to help you get a better grip on our economic problems. Take a look for yourself and see which of these myths you fell for:

Myth: The bailout will only help those on Wall Street, not people living on Main Street.

Reality: Although Wall Street firms have lost the trust of taxpayers, our economy depends on them. The bailout isn't made to "help" any one specific person directly but to help maintain the lifestyle of all Americans. It means keeping your bank accounts, loans, small business, insurance, and job in place. It means keeping your life in place.

Myth: The entire economic crisis is former President Bush's fault.

Reality: Although it would be easy to point the finger at a single person, the fact is the economic crisis has been coming for longer than just eight years. Democrats and Republicans alike pushed changes to regulations that governed financial institutions. In addition, I would not solely blame improper loan companies or even the corporations that needed bailing out. This is a deep-rooted crisis caused by dozens, if not hundreds, of mistakes that could have been prevented.

Myth: The bailout was supposed to provide immediate relief.

Reality: Back in early 2009, while the country watched as more jobs were lost and the stock market continued to fall, people were wondering why the bailout was not yet working. The truth is, the U.S. Treasury Department wasn't planning on doing the bulk of the spending until 2010 and 2011.

Myth: The bailout will fix the housing problem.

Reality: Much like Charlie Brown when Lucy keeps pulling away the football, we keep getting suckered by this gambit. Several government and industry programs have been designed to reverse the housing bust, slow the ballooning foreclosure rate, and keep more homeowners in their homes. None have worked on a large scale. There's a reason: this is an extraordinarily difficult problem to solve.

As many as five to ten million mortgages may still be at risk of foreclosure. Workouts and loan modifications may help save a small portion of them, but the vast majority of troubled mortgages aren't held by the banks that issued them. These are the mortgages that have been broken into components, bundled into securities (now derided as *toxic assets*), and sold to investors around the world. To renegotiate any one of those mortgages requires the participation of multiple parties, including some who will lose money and expect to be compensated. Now, multiply that by five million.

Myth: Why bail industries out? The sooner they fall, the sooner we recover.

Reality: Although this could work, the downside is that if it does not, we will all be in the hole. As I said earlier in this chapter, unfortunately, this country is not just relying on itself, and a pretty big chunk of our debt lies with foreign investors who are not very impressed with the situation. If those investors decide to pull their funds from American investments, then the economy could get much worse.

Quotes of Note on the Economic Collapse

The long-term budget projections are just horrifying, I've got four children and it really disturbs me. I just think it's irresponsible what we're doing to them.

— LEONARD BURMAN,
CO-DIRECTOR OF TAX POLICY FOR THE URBAN INSTITUTE

*During this coming economic depression, which has already
begun, the quality of life in major cities throughout American
[sic] will fall so far so fast it will take your breath away.*

—MICHAEL HAGA,

EDITOR, *THE ECONOMIC OUTLOOK*

*Below the favorable surface of the economy, there are as many
dangers and intractable circumstances as I can remember.
Nothing in our experience is comparable. We are consuming
about 6 percent more than we are producing. What holds
the [currency] together is the massive flows of capital from
abroad. A big adjustment will inevitably become necessary
long before Social Security surpluses disappear and the deficit
explodes. We are skating on increasingly thin ice.*

—PAUL VOLCKER,

FORMER CHAIRMAN OF THE FEDERAL RESERVE

*I am more disturbed than I have ever been in my investment
life about what lies ahead, the American consumer has driven
the world and the American consumer is out of gas and he is
also involved in a housing bubble that puts his very dwelling at
risk, and it worries me about what lies ahead because I don't
see any easy way out.*

—JULIAN ROBERTSON,

EX-CHAIRMAN OF TIGER MANAGEMENT,

THE WORLD'S LARGEST HEDGE FUND

*If you have billions and billions of dollars coming due in a
country in a short period of time, and if a sense of panic
develops among your creditors, so that everybody demands
the money out all at once, it's almost inevitable that the debtor*

*economy will collapse, because it won't be able to come up
with that amount of money in a short period.*

—Jeffrey Sachs,
American economist

This grim outlook includes Americans of all stripes, especially the eighty million or so who invest in stocks and real estate. The U.S. Government—aided and abetted by their allies on Wall Street, in academia, and in mass media—played the ultimate con game on the American people by encouraging them to continue borrowing money and consuming goods and services at a record pace.

Rampant consumerism, adrift from the production values that made America so powerful in the twentieth century, and the rise of competitive foreign nations like China and India have paved the way for the dramatic collapse of the U.S. economy and, consequently, a decline in the traditional American way of life.

How Will the IRS
Solve Its Cash Problem?
By Coming After You

You don't pay taxes—they take taxes.

—CHRIS ROCK

Even while our economy stumbles, our government keeps spending more. We know that we can't just print money to cover our bills. And look, the government's plans sound great. Who doesn't want to see some serious health care reform and improvements to our energy policy? But the money has to come from somewhere.

From a tax point of view, I think the government has really gone off the beam. Simply put, America needs a lot of money. We have major deficits and are not going to collect enough revenue to pay for all of it. The way things are going, before long, we'll all be drowning in higher taxes.

That's right. Despite what our leaders keep telling us, it's not just the top 1 percent of earners, and not just the people making a few hundred thousand dollars a year who will be paying. We will all be saddled with more taxes. With more than a trillion dollars in government spending, we could tax the top wage earners back to the Stone Age and still not come close to paying for all this spending. Without question, to pay for the 2008–2009 federal government spending spree, Congress is going to have to raise taxes across the board.

That, or we can all learn to speak Mandarin, because our only other option is to have an economically stronger country, like China, buy all our Treasury bonds, essentially purchasing our economy and everything that goes with it.

You think that's hyperbole? Not so much. Sure, ultimately all this bailout money might work. Of course, the downside is that if it does not, we will all be in the hole. Unfortunately, the United States isn't exactly self-sufficient these days, because a pretty big chunk of our debt lies with foreign investors who are not very impressed with the situation. If those investors decide to pull their funds from American investments, then the economy could get much worse.

How can the government raise more money in a fair and equitable fashion? Well, if I were queen of the world, I would change the way the government conducts its finances. Right now, we're behaving like a teenage shopaholic with Daddy's credit card, and that has to stop. The trouble is that our options are limited: we can reduce spending or borrow money (until we finally manage to grow trees that produce money). Currently, 15 to 20 percent of taxpayers cannot pay their bills, so raising taxes on those people will be difficult. We need to think about reducing spending in a balanced way so our schools are healthy, our national security is solid, our small businesses can grow, and our police, fire, and hospital budgets aren't slashed to pieces.

What Does It All Mean?

It's not just about an inevitable increase in taxes. The trillion-dollar bailout of 2009 and the shrinking number of Americans who actually pay income taxes ensure that the IRS will get even more aggressive about collecting back taxes from beleaguered taxpayers.

With more than $12 trillion of debt and "only" $1.1 trillion in new taxes to offset our increasing debts, the federal government can only raise money to pay off the debt in three ways:

1. Issue bonds on the global fixed income market (on which we have to pay interest).
2. Print more money (and thus reduce the value of the dollar, and trigger a run-up in inflation).
3. Come after you, the taxpayer, for more money in the form of even higher taxes and aggressive pursuit of money owed in back taxes.

As I've mentioned, there is no guarantee that current U.S. Treasury bondholders like China and India will keep investing in America by loaning us money through the purchase of bonds. The second option

Almost Half of Americans Don't Pay Income Taxes

In 2009, approximately 47 percent of households did not owe any federal income tax, according to estimates by the nonpartisan Tax Policy Center. The Center adds that some in that group will even get additional money from the government because they qualify for refundable tax breaks.

The number of those whose major federal tax burdens net out at zero—or less—is on the rise. The center's original 2009 estimate was 38 percent. That was before enactment of the $787 billion economic recovery package, which included a host of new or expanded tax breaks.

"It is time for a serious public discussion of whether it is desirable to have so many Americans disconnected from the cost of government and what the consequences are of using the tax system as a vehicle for social policy," writes Scott Hodge of the Tax Foundation.

is completely untenable—you can't just print more currency and not expect disaster in the form of a weaker dollar and rampant inflation.

That leaves taxes, and the frightening prospect of the federal government getting more aggressive in raising taxes on individuals and companies, and becoming more vigilant about tracking down Americans who owe back taxes and forcing them to cough it up. Think about it: a government addicted to tax monies will stop at nothing to get its fix. The same government that twisted Swiss banks' arms to get them to release the names of account holders will have no problem coming after you if you owe Uncle Sam a few thousand—or even hundred—bucks.

With millions of jobs lost and more than two million homes lost to foreclosure in 2009 alone, people are hurting out there. The last thing they need is to be hunted down by the IRS, then held upside down by the ankles to have the rest of their money shaken out of their pockets.

If you have a debt with the IRS, rest assured, it will come looking for you, no matter how big or small your tax debt may be.

In fact, it's already started. In 2009, IRS agents collected $59.2 billion in investigations and collections—a new record. At every level, the IRS has become increasingly aggressive in pursuing tax cheats. The tax collecting agency is not only going after those U.S. taxpayers who try to avoid taxes but also their alleged enablers—people who promote tax shelters or otherwise help them keep their money from the U.S. government.

Taxes Going Up

With all of the wild government spending, what's the fallout going to look like? For starters, Bush administration tax cuts for the highest-earning taxpayers, such as families earning more than $250,000 a year, would be allowed to expire in 2011. The highest income tax rate would revert to 36 percent for individuals and 39.6 percent for married couples, from the current high of 35 percent.

Capital gains taxes on the highest-earning Americans would increase to 20 percent from the current 15 percent.

Under President Obama's plan, a single person with no children earning $500,000 in household income would pay an additional $19,200 in taxes. A married couple with the same income and two children under seventeen would see a tax increase of $11,300.

Taxing "Illegal" Income

Every so often, I hear someone complain that with so much coming out of their income in taxes, they would be better off being a criminal. At least then they could keep whatever they earn, right? Well, in these times, you might not want to quit your day job.

According to the IRS, illegal income is also taxable income. Often, the IRS only becomes aware of the illegal income after an arrest is made, so once the criminal trial is over, the IRS comes looking for its share.

It is rather hilarious to think of criminals diligently reporting the proceeds of their illegal activities, but this is what the IRS actually requires.

What about Businesses?

Many businesses will also see their taxes rise. The administration wants to raise about $210 billion over ten years by tightening tax enforcement for U.S. companies with international operations and tax policy reforms.

Oil and gas companies will see their taxes rise about $31.5 billion over a decade as the administration eliminates various tax preferences and places an excise tax on drilling in the Gulf of Mexico.

Another big change would affect hedge funds whose managers' incomes are now taxed at the lower capital gains rate of 15 percent.

Obama would make their earnings taxable at the ordinary income tax rate, raising $23.9 billion over ten years.

Then there's the health care issue, where individuals and companies may be fined if they don't enroll in a plan or offer health care to employees.

And administration officials estimate the cap-and-trade system that the administration would implement to reduce businesses'

U.S. Federal Budget: $3 Trillion in New Taxes over the Next Ten Years (Starting in 2011)

According to the *Wall Street Journal*, President Obama's budget proposes $3 trillion in new taxes over the course of the next ten years, starting fiscal year 2011, most of which are tax increases on individuals.

1. On people making more than $250,000:

   - $700 billion—Bush tax cuts expire. These are the tax cuts on businesses and individuals that end in 2010.
   - $291 billion—cap on itemized deductions. These taxes would come from reducing the amount of some itemized deductions, such as mortgage interest and charitable donations, for higher-income taxpayers.
   - $24 billion—capital gains tax hike. This tax would hit investors and businesses hard. The less investors get for taking risk on stocks, the less money businesses will have for things like hiring, product development, and research.
   - An additional $10 billion budget for IRS to enforce the New Health Care Reform.
   - An actual increase of U.S. health care spending to $311 trillion over the next ten years.

Source: http://money.cnn.com/2010/02/01/pf/taxes/obama_budget_tax_changes/

greenhouse gas emissions—although not technically a tax—would raise $645.7 billion over ten years.

What about Small Businesses?

Republicans and other critics, knowing they will get little mileage from defending the rich, are casting the plan as a tax hit on people

2. Businesses:

- $19 billion—Reinstate Superfund taxes
- $24 billion—tax investment managers' "carried interest" as regular income
- $10 billion—codify "economic substance doctrine"
- $59.1 billion—repeal LIFO
- $210 billion—international enforcement, reform deferral, and other tax reform
- $4 billion—information reporting for rental payments
- $5.3 billion—excise tax on Gulf of Mexico oil and gas
- $3.4 billion—repeal expensing of tangible drilling costs
- $62 million—repeal deduction for tertiary injectants
- $49 million—repeal passive loss exception for working interests in oil and natural gas properties
- $13 billion—repeal manufacturing tax deduction for oil and natural gas companies
- $1 billion—increase to seven years geological and geophysical amortization period for independent producers
- $882 million—eliminate advanced earned income tax credit

Total: $353 billion/ten years
Combined Total: $989 billion
Source: ABC News

who run industrious little companies driving job growth. But that's not likely, according to one in-depth analysis, which found that more than 95 percent of small business owners would be off the hook.

President Obama's plan does not propose higher business taxes. But critics reason that owners of many small companies report business income on their personal tax returns instead of filing corporate taxes. That exposes their business earnings to Obama's higher tax rates on the wealthy. To be sure, some business owners would get caught in that net.

However, many small businesses with employees don't earn enough to put their owners over the threshold for the higher tax rates. In fact, in 2009, the Tax Policy Center (run jointly by the Urban Institute and Brookings Institution) examined the likely effects of Obama's plans to raise taxes on couples making more than $250,000. Their analysis estimated that 663,000 taxpayers who report business income or losses fall in the two tax brackets whose rates would go up under Obama's plan. That is roughly 5 percent of the small businesses in the country.

What was the reaction to the tax changes specified or implied by the president's budget? Liberal advocacy groups welcomed the changes and praised the budget for addressing health care and global warming.

Congressional Republicans decried the changes, saying raising taxes on the highest-income earners would harm small businesses and job creation, especially during a time of deep recession. Business groups said the tax package would delay a long-awaited economic recovery.

Marty Regalia, the chief economist at the U.S. Chamber of Commerce, called Obama's tax proposals "the biggest return to the welfare state that we've seen in decades."

Senator Judd Gregg (R-NH), who withdrew his nomination as

Obama's commerce secretary-designate over differences with the president on the stimulus, said the cap-and-trade program would affect everyone in the country.

"You've got a tax on people's electric bills here. Everybody who gets an electric bill in this country who happens to be in a region where there are coal-fired plants or other plants subject to a carbon limitation tax, they're going to be getting a big tax on their energy bills," Gregg said.

"The government tried to raise taxes once before in a recession," stated Republican House Leader John Boehner. "It was in 1932. And all that did was make our recession a whole lot worse. Everyone agrees that all Americans ought to have access to affordable health insurance. But increasing taxes in the middle of an economic recession, especially on small businesses, is not the way to accomplish that goal."

Government, Heal Thyself

Jeez Louise! You'd think the federal government would set the standard in being a financial role model for U.S. taxpayers.

Fat chance. It turns out that public employees are at the top of the list of taxpayers who owe money to Uncle Sam.

In December 2009, more than 276,300 federal employees and retirees owed a total of $3 billion in back taxes, according to Senate Finance Committee Chairman Max Baucus (D-MT) and ranking Republican Chuck Grassley (R-IA).

"Of all people, Federal workers should pay their Federal taxes on time," said Senator Baucus in a press release. "If the government doesn't make its own employees follow the rules, it's hard to tell the rest of the American people that they should do better. The president should make his expectations clear to every worker on the federal payroll. This is one simple way the administration can tackle the problem of taxes owed but unpaid without an act of Congress and without additional burdens on law-abiding taxpayers."

Former President George Bush wrote a letter to Senators Baucus and Grassley, in which he stated, "One of the strongest features of our democracy is our system of collecting income taxes through individual self-assessment. The American public rightly expects a high degree of honesty and personal integrity from those in government. And those in government have a duty and responsibility to assure the American public they have the highest ethical standards and are paying their fair share of taxes."

I don't want to pick on federal employees, who, by and large, are good workers and solid citizens. But at a time when the federal government is getting aggressive about going after taxpayers, it's troubling to know it has failed to clean out its own backyard first. When top politicians like Treasury Secretary Tim Geithner, former Democratic Senator Tom Daschle, and current Chairman of the powerful House Ways and Means Committee Charles Rangel don't pay their taxes, why should the rest of us?

Why Do Most People Fall Behind on Taxes?

People get behind the tax eight ball for a lot of reasons, but some of those reasons are more common than others.

Anyone who knows me knows that I'm a straight shooter. So if you fall behind on your taxes for reasons other than financial hardship, you need to get your act together. The price is way too high— the IRS will come after you and won't stop until either you fight back or pay up. You don't want that grief in your life.

Here's a list of common reasons that otherwise conscientious people get behind on their taxes. As you'll notice, some of the reasons I've listed, like failure to file, are entirely avoidable, even in tough economic times.

Failure to File

You'd be surprised by the number of people who just don't file their taxes. But this one is a no-brainer—filing taxes is the law of the land. Even so, one of the most common mistakes a taxpayer can make is failing to file a tax return. I tell my clients all the time: if you live and earn income in the United States (above a minimum threshold) during a particular year, you are probably required to pay taxes and report that income by filing a federal tax return.

From what I see at my law firm, a lot of taxpayers are either uninformed or wrongly informed that they don't have tax filing obligations. But they really perk up when I tell them that failing to file can lead to penalties and interest being assessed that could lead to a big tax bill. Additionally, the more delinquent tax returns you have, the higher your tax liability, penalties, and interest will be.

Substitute for Returns

If you are required to file but fail to do so, the IRS can file a Substitute for Return on your behalf. A Substitute for Return is a tax return prepared by the IRS based on any information it may have for you (W-2s, 1099s, etc.). By and large, that means the IRS is using a filing status of "single" with a household of one, which ignores any eligible deductions, credits, and additional exemptions that you may be able to claim. The Substitute for Return will then calculate how much is owed and, believe me, the IRS will come after you for it.

Wage Earners—Underwithholding

You've probably heard of this one before. By law, employers typically withhold taxes from your paycheck. But if enough taxes are not withheld from your paycheck to cover your tax liabilities, you can end up with an overwhelming tax bill in April. The IRS calls this *underwithholding*. It usually results from an employee claiming too many exemptions on their Form W-4—which you probably completed when you were hired and then failed to change as you have received increases, added members to your household or deductible expenses, etc.

Self-Employed—Fail to Make Estimated Tax Payments

My fellow business owners and entrepreneurs often get into trouble by not making estimated tax payments. When you are self-employed, taxes are not automatically withheld from your income, so the IRS expects you to pay up on a quarterly or monthly basis. If you don't, you end up with a huge tax bill, in addition to IRS penalties. Unfortunately, many self-employed taxpayers, being ultra-busy people, are not aware of their reporting and payment obligations until it is too late.

Additional Triggers

It's not just self-employed taxpayers—everyone's busy these days. Consequently, some other reasons people may owe the IRS are directly linked to what's going on in their personal lives. For example, a taxpayer may have a family crisis or an emergency that occurs around tax season that prevents the taxpayer from filing a tax return on time or prevents the taxpayer from paying his or her tax bill in full. In that kind of situation, the IRS will issue the taxpayer a bill for the amount owed.

Other taxpayers may simply misunderstand the tax laws and take exemptions, deductions, and credits that they are not qualified to claim. In this situation, the IRS will usually contact the taxpayer and inform him or her of the reporting error. The taxpayer is then required to substantiate the exemption, deduction, or credit taken.

File . . . Because I Said So!

What are the criteria for filing? Well, things change on a nearly annual basis, but here's a good rule of thumb.

To determine if you have to file a return, the IRS uses three criteria: your age, your filing status, and your income. Generally, once you reach a certain income level, the law requires you to file. The amounts are adjusted annually for inflation. Now, of course, the numbers the IRS uses to determine whether or not you need to file a tax return change each year, so you have to be really in tune with the IRS's flavor of the year—each year—when it comes to filing your tax returns. For example, take the difference between the 2008 and 2009 filing figures.

Individuals younger than age sixty-five must file if they make at least:

- Single filers: $9,350 in 2009; $8,950 in 2008
- Head of household filers: $12,000 in 2009; $11,500 in 2008
- Married filing jointly: $18,700 in 2009; $17,900 in 2008

The earnings threshold amounts go up a bit for older (sixty-five plus) individuals:

- Single filers: $10,750 in 2009; $10,300 in 2008
- Head of household filer: $13,400 in 2009; $12,850 in 2008
- Married filing jointly with one spouse older than sixty-five: $19,800 in 2009; $18,950 in 2008
- Married filing jointly and both spouses are older than sixty-five: $20,900 in 2009; $20,000 in 2008

The earnings target is the same—$3,650—for married couples filing separately, regardless of age. However, this figure was $3,500 in 2008.

Even if you don't have a tax filing requirement for a given tax year, I think it's in your best interest to file a tax return because you may have had taxes withheld or might qualify for tax credits, which could result in a refund to you. That's one of the Tax Lady's favorite phrases: "IRS tax rule in your favor!"

Without substantiation, the IRS will correct the tax return and the taxpayer may end up with a hefty tax liability, maybe even penalties and interest.

What Happens if I Owe?

Of course, the best way to handle tax debt is to avoid it altogether by being diligent in your tax filing and paying. But if it's too late for prevention, then you must be prepared for battle.

If the IRS thinks you owe past-due taxes, it is not shy about getting hold of you. Almost always, the IRS sends you an ominous bill in the mail. Sometimes it reaches out to you with a phone call. In serious cases, it may even visit you at work or at home. If the IRS is unable to get you to satisfy your tax debt voluntarily, it may take collection action (i.e., liens, levies, garnishments, and property seizures) against you. In any case, you are almost guaranteed to be on the hook for additional interest and penalties while your debt remains outstanding.

Strong-Arm Tactics Don't Always Feed the Beast

Taxpayer advocate Nina Olson points out that even though the IRS has aggressively stepped up its collection efforts, such aggressiveness hasn't translated into a commensurate amount of money in the U.S. Treasury's tax coffers.

Olson notes that although enforced collection actions like the authority to levy and seizure are important collection tools that allow the IRS to address serious incidents of noncompliance, a review of IRS historical enforcement data shows that more enforcement actions do not translate into commensurate increases in revenue collection. Here's one example: the number of levies issued by the IRS increased by 1,608 percent between 2000 and 2007—from 220,000 levies to about 3.76 million levies—yet the increase in the total collection yield during the period was slightly less than 45 percent. By contrast, historical enforcement data indicate that collection alternatives, such as Offers in Compromise and Installment Agreements, may be more effective at collecting liabilities from taxpayers who have difficulty paying their tax debts.

Roni's Soapbox

I mentioned earlier in this chapter how badly the deck is stacked tax-wise against the average American.

You've read the facts as I have laid them out and I am sure you are in agreement with my conclusion. In this economy, with one out of five people either out of work or just working part-time, there's just not enough income floating around these days for regular folks to handle the nation's tax burden.

But because that tax burden is going to grow even heavier in the coming years, our government will force us to bear the financial brunt. It has no other choice. With our total national debt of more than $11 trillion and added costs linked to government programs like Medicare, Social Security, health care reform, and possibly even cap-and-trade energy regulations, we're on a fast track to a significantly harsher tax landscape.

So, in the end, Uncle Sam is going to get his money—no matter how much it makes the U.S. taxpayer bleed. That's why it's vital that taxpayers learn about ways that the IRS plans on coming after them for its extra pounds of flesh.

More importantly, taxpayers need to learn ways to stop the bloodthirsty beasts in Washington from grabbing more of their hard-earned cash.

3

How Will the IRS Come After You? Let Me Count the Ways

Addiction: To devote or surrender (oneself) to something habitually or obsessively

I 've often compared the U.S. government to a drug addict, and it's a comparison I don't make lightly.

I have tremendous sympathy for people who suffer from addiction, because they want to get better, but they often don't know how to do so.

In the government's case, the addiction to tax money is so deep and so permanent that I don't believe that politicians *want* to get better.

To paraphrase Christopher Walken's cowbell-crazy rock producer on *Saturday Night Live* years back, the government has a fever—and the only cure is more taxes.

Study after study shows that every dollar taken in taxes is one more dollar taken directly from the economy. Worse, if that tax dollar is sent to China to pay back creditors who bought our U.S.

Treasury bonds, then the economy becomes even weaker. It's in this fashion that the U.S. government has become completely addicted to tax revenues at the expense of the economy. The only way to get an addict off drugs is to put him in rehab and let him go through withdrawal. The same is true with the government: if you take away the money raised through tax bingeing, then you force the government to go through withdrawal.

Take the recent economic collapse. The U.S. government depends on the good health of the economy, and a recession reduces tax revenues, which, unless spending is cut, plunges us right back into deficits. Adding more fuel to the fire is the tendency in Washington to hike government spending during recessions in order to boost the economy.

Talk about enabling a drug addict.

Government Spending Breeds Big Appetite for Taxes

It's no secret that when the federal government's reach expands—as it is doing right now—Americans will face higher taxes.

The most recent data shows that more than half of all Americans (52.6 percent) receive significant income from government programs, according to an analysis by Gary Shilling, an economist in Springfield, New Jersey. That's up from 49.4 percent in 2000 and far above the 28.3 percent of Americans in 1950.

Shilling's analysis revealed a number of findings:

- One in five Americans holds a government job or a job reliant on federal spending.
- A similar number receive Social Security or a government pension.
- About nineteen million others get food stamps, two million get subsidized housing, and five million get education grants.

- The Congressional Budget Office, in a long-range forecast prepared in 2005, outlined a baseline scenario in which entitlement programs push federal spending to 25.3 percent of GDP by mid-century, up from about 18.4 percent today. That number could go higher still if medical inflation doesn't edge downward.

Similarly, Shilling predicts that the number of "government beneficiaries," as he defines them, will grow to 60 percent of the U.S. population by 2040. And one of the main ways to pay for all of those government programs is by making hard-working taxpayers like you and me pay more in taxes. Against this backdrop, many Americans are understandably uneasy about the fiscal path of their politicians.

How Are They Gonna Get You?

To understand how brutal the IRS can be, the most appropriate comparison would be the world's largest collection agency. After all, both the IRS and your garden-variety collection agency operate under similar rules and collection measures. Think about it:

They're not in existence for humanitarian reasons; both collection agencies and the IRS exist to part you from your money. Both will stop at nothing to get your money, and the last thing each is worried about is your privacy and your dignity.

Both operate on the margins (outside the margins, I would argue) of civilized human decency, unless you consider constant phone calls, registered letters, wage garnishments, and threats against your home and credit to be civilized human decency.

So how exactly is the IRS going to come after you if you have tax debt? Well, like the world's worst collection agency, the IRS has a few swift and brutal methods for getting your attention if it thinks you owe it money.

At first, it may seem innocuous enough. Although nobody is thrilled with a registered letter from the IRS, at least the average tax collection notice doesn't threaten to take your home and/or bank account—yet. Here's a rundown of two of the most common IRS notices:

1. **Proposed Individual Tax Assessment (Letter 2566 SC/ CG)**

   The Proposed Individual Tax Assessment is also referred to as a thirty-day letter. This letter notifies you that the IRS has no record of receiving your Form 1040, U.S. Individual Income Tax Return.

   It proposes a tax assessment with penalties and interest based on income reported to the IRS by your employers, banks, etc.

   The letter also states that within thirty days, you must submit one of the following:

   - Your Form 1040 completed and signed, including all schedules and forms with cover letter.
   - The Consent to Assessment and Collection form, signed and dated.
   - A statement explaining why you believe you are not required to file, or information you would like the IRS to consider.

2. **Notice of Deficiency (Letter 3219 SC/CG)**

   A Notice of Deficiency is sometimes referred to as a ninety-day letter. The Notice of Deficiency tells you the tax assessed plus the interest and penalties you will owe.

   A Notice of Deficiency is required by law and is to advise you of your appeal rights to the U.S. Tax Court.

   The letter also states that within ninety days, you must submit one of the following:

- Your Form 1040 completed and signed, including all schedules and forms with cover letter.
- The Consent to Assessment and Collection form, signed and dated.
- A statement explaining why you believe you are not required to file, or information you would like the IRS to consider.

Source: Internal Revenue Service

Sometimes, the IRS sends a second letter or notice requesting additional information or providing additional information to you. Be sure to keep copies of any correspondence with your records.

When IRS collection notices are ignored, the IRS resorts to enforced collections. Take it from me: enforced collections are the "weapons of mass destruction" for collection purposes. It is what makes the IRS the most powerful collection agency in the world.

The most common IRS tax collection tools are the bank levy and the wage levy. If you receive notice from the IRS that either type of levy is going to be issued on you, you need to act fast. This is your money on the line! The IRS also commonly uses tax liens as a passive method of collections; however, they can sometimes ripen into a seizure of the underlying asset.

Bank Levy: The IRS bank levy is a nasty but thoroughly effective method of grabbing your money to satisfy back taxes. Trust me when I say lots of financial lives have been ruined over bank levies. Here's how it goes down:

1. The IRS freezes your bank account.
2. Three weeks—that's how much time the IRS gives you to contact them and explain why you should be spared a bank levy. If you don't respond or if you cannot give the IRS a

compelling reason to release the bank levy, the IRS will take and keep every cent in your account.

If you get a Notice of Intent to Levy from the IRS, don't procrastinate. You're up against the wall, so bring in a tax professional if possible. You don't have much time and a tax professional has a better chance of negotiating with the IRS and getting the bank levy eliminated within that three-week timetable. The stakes are high— once Uncle Sam gets hold of your cash, chances are you won't get your money back.

Wage Levy: Got a job? That's great news in the eyes of the IRS, because it can legally swoop in and grab your paycheck before you ever see a dime. It's called a wage levy or garnishment, and it's even more painfully effective than a bank levy. By and large, the IRS can take a percentage of your paycheck until your tax debt is paid in full or until the statute of limitations on your tax debt expires. By law, the IRS can snag 70 percent of your paycheck. Like with a bank levy, time is of the essence. Get a grip and take action before Uncle Sam grabs your paycheck.

Tax Lien on Your Home: I'll have a lot more to say about tax liens in chapter 4, but the IRS can also "freeze" your home by placing a tax lien on it. That means you can't sell it until the lien is satisfied. A tax lien on your home will not only scare off potential buyers, it's a huge black mark on your credit score. Once the IRS sends a notice threatening a tax lien, you have three weeks (exactly) to contact the IRS and plead your case. A good tax professional may be able to avoid the lien and get you on an installment plan, but you have to act fast.

IRS Seizures: The IRS can also seize your home, your income, your paycheck, and other valuable assets and property, then turn around and sell it at an auction to cover your tax debt. If you own a business, the IRS can even seize that, including bank accounts, leased vehicles, and any commercial property you own.

Steps to Avoid Owing Back Taxes

Other than a root canal, I can't imagine a worse situation than owing the IRS. Why? Because the IRS is so much more powerful than any other debt collector; it is able to slap you with high penalties and fees that can drastically increase your total liability. The good news is—and rest assured, the Tax Lady *always* has good news—with a little bit of foresight, organization, and observation, you can avoid getting into the mud with the IRS.

1. **Adjust Withholdings**
    As an employee, you can change your withholdings at any time by filing a new Form W-4 with your human resources department. It's usually a good idea to use the Goldilocks approach to withholdings—not too much and not too little. If you withhold too much, you are giving the federal government an interest-free loan; too little and you are going to have to cut a fat check, and possibly pay a penalty, come April 15th. Nobody wants that.

2. **Make Your Estimated Tax Payments**
    By the same token, self-employed taxpayers must make estimated tax payments. Unfortunately, the historical failure of small business owners to make timely and accurate estimated tax payments has led the IRS to keep a close eye on all small business owners. If you are required to make estimated tax payments, then it is now more important than ever to make sure you make them on time.

3. **Follow the Rules**
    The worst possible mistake you can make while filing a tax return is claiming a deduction for which you do not qualify.

At my tax firm, we see a lot of taxpayers make the mistake of assuming that they qualify for deductions, credits, and exemptions for which they do not. One good example of this is the child tax credit; although it seems like anyone with a kid should get the credit, there are a lot of qualifications of which you may not be aware. Always double- and triple-check any large exemptions or credits.

4. **When in Doubt, Ask a Professional**

    If you are ever not sure about your taxes, from how much to withhold to how many exemptions to claim on your returns, ask a professional. Although you might not relish the thought of paying someone to look at your taxes, I promise, the expense is minor when compared to how much a mistake can cost you.

Kick You When You're Already Down

Although levies and liens are the most formidable weapons in the IRS's tax-collecting arsenal, they're not the only ones.

Let's summarize some of these tactics right here. I'll elaborate on them in subsequent chapters:

Home Sweet Home—In chapter 4, I'll talk about how your home may be at risk if you owe the IRS money. I will also examine how walking away from your home could lead to a large tax bill down the road.

Will Work for Food—In chapter 5, I'll address how your job situation or lack of a job could be affected by tax debt. Just being out of work and down on your luck doesn't entitle you to a get-out-of-jail-free card when it comes to paying your taxes, at least not according to the IRS.

I'm the Boss—In chapter 6, we go entrepreneurial (something I know a little bit about), and I'll explain how your small business can be impacted by tax debt. The IRS will not go easy on you just because you had a slow month.

Personal Crisis—In chapter 7, I'll cover the consequences that personal crises like divorce, a death in the family, bankruptcy, or a major health setback can have.

Your Investments—If you're in tax trouble with the IRS and have investments or a retirement plan, you better believe the IRS will target your personal financial portfolio. That's the focus of chapter 8.

If You Think You Have Problems . . .

I see people every day who owe $10,000 or $20,000 in back taxes. Make no mistake, that's a lot of money to the average taxpayer, and neither I nor anyone else who works for me takes that lightly. Here's something that can help to put your tax grief in perspective. After all, can you imagine owing $2.6 million in back taxes? That's what entertainer Dionne Warwick owed the IRS back in 2007.

Flip the calendar back to 1991, when the IRS sold country singer Willie Nelson's home and possessions (even forcing him to release a new album) to help settle a $16.7 million tax bill.

A number of other celebrities have owed back taxes in recent years:

- Dick Morris—This former political adviser to Bill Clinton is a bestselling book author and frequent media political commentator. But he had tax problems, too. The IRS filed a $1.5 million tax lien against him in 2003. The state of Connecticut reports Morris owed $452,367 in back taxes and penalties.
- Sinbad—The comedian and actor owed $2.1 million to the state of California, according to the California Franchise Tax Board. In addition, the IRS slapped a $416,870 tax lien against him in 2006.

- Catalina Vásquez Villalpando—The former treasurer of the United States—her signature appears on paper currency printed during the administration of the first President Bush—owed $168,000 in taxes to Washington, DC. Villalpando was convicted of tax evasion in 1994 for shielding money from the IRS. She eventually served four months in prison.
- Nicolas Cage—The actor owes the IRS more than $14 million in back taxes; the IRS filed a tax lien for more than $6.2 million against Cage in July 2009. The actor has been selling off his mansions and other property around the world in an effort to pay off the tax lien.
- Eve—This rapper owes in excess of $357,000 in back state and federal taxes. In January 2008, the IRS in LA filed two liens against her, one for $242,245 and another for $56,597. In January 2009, that same branch filed two additional liens against Eve, one for $29,439 and other for $29,059.
- Snoop Dogg—The IRS filed a $598,309 tax lien against the thirty-eight-year old rapper in January 2010.

Source: *USA Today*, April 17, 2008

I don't single out celebrities to make light of their plight. I do so to make a point. You can have all the fame, all the money, and the best hair stylist in Beverly Hills, but you can still owe the IRS a lot of money, and it will come after you.

Every Step You Take, They'll Be Watching You

In 2009, the IRS collected $48.9 billion, which represents a 13 percent decrease in collections from 2008, when the IRS collected $56.4 billion. Although the amount collected in 2009 decreased, the level of enforced collection actually increased. The number of liens issued by the IRS increased approximately 25 percent, from 768,168 in 2008 to 965,618 in 2009. Likewise, the number of levies issued by the IRS increased approximately 32 percent, from 2,631,038 in 2008 to 4,478,181 in 2009.

The IRS certainly isn't shy about getting what it believes it is owed. Collecting those billions of dollars required the IRS to issue more than 2.6 million tax levies (including wage garnishments and bank levies) and 760,000 tax liens on taxpayers' property.

Tax levies and liens normally occur after several notices from the IRS. Taxpayers can avoid the horror of levies and liens by taking swift action and negotiating with the IRS. In certain circumstances, penalties, interest, and even underlying tax liability can be significantly reduced by being proactive and resolving the debt.

How to Resolve a Tax Debt

One of the best ways to get past the tax debt blues is to be armed with the knowledge that there are ways to get relief. You have options available to help you work out a bearable tax debt solution. We'll get into more detail for each possible resolution in chapter 9, but here are some of the most commonly used and the most effective from a taxpayer point of view.

1. Offer in Compromise: An Offer in Compromise (OIC) is when the IRS agrees to settle your entire tax debt for a lesser amount. Will the agents at the IRS consider a compromise? Well, they're not going to agree happily, but it can be done. So if you cannot afford to pay the IRS fully but have some money set aside, try filing an OIC with the IRS. The OIC program is a good deal; if you qualify, your tax debt is eliminated for a lot less cash than you owe. How do you get an OIC? The IRS will want to see all your financial information, including how much you make, how much you have in cash and assets, and what your expenses are. Once the agents are satisfied that what you are offering is the best deal they can hope for, you send them the cash, and your debt is resolved.

2. Installment Agreement: If you can't afford to pay off your tax debt at once, and you don't qualify for an OIC but you *can* afford a monthly payment, then an Installment Agreement is your best option. Essentially, just like any payment plan, you agree to make monthly payments, reducing your tax liability until the debt is repaid or the debt expires.

How do you get an Installment Agreement? The IRS will want to see all your financial documents, because IRS payments are not based on how much you owe, but on how much you can afford to pay. Once you and the IRS agree on a monthly payment amount, just make the monthly payments.

3. Currently Not Collectible: If you owe the IRS and have absolutely nothing, it may classify you as Currently Not Collectible (CNC). Once you are placed on CNC status, the IRS halts all collection activity. You still have the tax debt, but the statute of limitations on your tax debt continues to run, and the IRS will leave you alone. You can stay on this protected status until your debt expires or until your financial situation improves enough to allow you to make a monthly payment.

How do you get placed on CNC status? Again, the IRS will want to see all your financial documents, your income, your expenses, and your assets. Once the agents are satisfied that you have nothing of value and cannot make payments, they can classify you as CNC and get off your back.

4. Personal Bankruptcy: Bankruptcy is tough, and the decision to file for it should never be taken lightly. But for some people, it can be a lifesaver. Depending on your bankruptcy chapter filing, you may be able to resolve your tax debt without losing everything you have.

In order to file for bankruptcy, you must work with a bankruptcy attorney. He or she can advise you of what chapter filing you should pursue and whether you can have your tax debts discharged. Just remember, this is not a get-out-of-jail-free card, and some tax debts cannot be resolved through any type of bankruptcy.

To beat the IRS, you need two things: a good plan and an insider's knowledge of how the IRS works. Those are two attributes that I've crafted, honed, and perfected in my two-plus decades as an IRS tax-fighting specialist.

Like I said, when you owe the IRS back taxes, you have to be ready for anything. The IRS has all these programs to help you get out of trouble, but if you don't know how the game is played, the agency will take advantage of you every time.

4

Lien on Me: How the IRS Attacks Your Home

A house is made of walls and beams, a home is built
with love and dreams, but in an instant the IRS can take
both by filing a lien.

—Anonymous

There's an old saying that it takes hands to build a house, but it takes a heart to build a home. I know, I love my home, too. Unfortunately, when it comes to taxes, the IRS also loves your home. In fact, IRS agents love it so much they'll threaten to take it away from you if you owe back taxes—either directly through a tax lien or indirectly through foreclosure.

Both are weapons that the government will load and aim at a moment's notice. Both are excruciatingly harmful. Tax liens and foreclosures not only ruin your credit score, threaten your retirement, and potentially set you back tens of thousands of dollars, they can also trigger so much financial destruction that it will take you years to get back to square one.

The notion of IRS agents elbowing everyone else out of the way, cutting in line, and slapping a lien on your home—thus guaranteeing that they will get paid first—really boils me. I mean, how dare they? How dare they come barging into our lives and our homes, waving ominous-looking packets filled with threats, and claim they can hold you up with a tax lien until you pay up?

Don't get me wrong. I've said it once and I'll say it again: lots of people who owe back taxes need to pay up. Those are the guys (and gals) who deliberately skip out on their taxes and wait for the IRS to catch up with them (and it always does).

But there are lots of innocent people who are brought to their financial knees because of an illness, a gut-wrenching divorce, and (especially in this economy) the loss of a job or the failure of a small business.

These are the folks I represent and they're good people. Their only mistake is a run of bad luck, and the last thing they need is the IRS perched vulture-like on their shoulders.

Your smart tax move is to figure out how to keep your home protected when you owe the IRS back taxes. There are two key "home" themes to review:

1. How to fight a tax lien.
2. How a home foreclosure can affect your taxes.

A federal tax lien is one of the most brutal and effective ways the IRS can come after you if you owe back taxes. And although you may think that your tax debt should have nothing to do with your personal property, the IRS will tell you to think again. If you have assets and you owe Uncle Sam, he's going to want a piece of the action.

In essence, a tax lien is a legal right or interest that the IRS, or any creditor, has in your property because of a debt you owe. The lien lasts until your debt is paid off or otherwise satisfied. Having a lien placed on your house can make it difficult to sell. Discovering the lien may scare off the buyer and some mortgage lenders will scoff at funding loans to buy property with a lien on it.

If the IRS is feeling nice, it may subordinate the lien, which means moving its interest in the property to a secondary position. The IRS will usually only do this so that you may sell or refinance the property with the proceeds going toward paying your tax debt. Of course, by repaying the debt, the lien is released.

Keep in mind the tax lien doesn't just cover the amount of back taxes you owe; it also includes interest, penalties, and any associated costs that may accrue while your debt is outstanding. Your tax bill can mushroom because of these additional costs, so resolving the debt before the lien is ever put in place is your best bet.

That's a no-brainer, right? But sometimes the best intentions get away from us, so what do you do if the IRS has filed a lien against your home? First, even though it's the federal government, the IRS still needs to play by the rules, and it helps if you know those rules, too.

Tax Lien Versus a Tax Seizure

A tax lien and a tax levy (or seizure) are actually quite different. It's the difference between the IRS setting the stage to take your assets away—and actually taking them away.

In a word, a tax lien is a legal charge on property. For instance, a tax lien could include your home or even your new car. A levy is the real-life seizure of assets. In essence, a tax lien does not seize anything; it "encumbers" assets (by law, *all* your assets). A tax levy is the actual seizure of those assets.

Before the IRS can even file a Notice of Federal Tax Lien, it has to do several things:

1. The IRS should first assess your tax liability;
2. Then the IRS needs to send you a Notice and Demand for Payment notifying you of the taxes owed;

3. It must give you ten days to pay your tax debt in full after being notified.

If you don't comply, a lien may be filed for the amount owed. Once the lien is filed, the IRS has five business days to tell you in writing, which should include a "Notice of Right to Request a Hearing." A hearing is your chance to dispute the lien. If you request a hearing, it must occur within thirty-six days of the lien's filing. This gives you some time to prepare your defense. If at the end of the hearing you win on appeal, then the lien is withdrawn, but it will still show up on your credit report. If you don't win, you will have to begin proceedings to work out a payment of your tax debt.

Once the lien is filed, a public notice is given to creditors that the IRS has a claim against your property. This is done to establish priority of debt and who gets paid in case of bankruptcy or sale of the property.

Don't think that the lien is solely against your house, either. Legally, the lien attaches to all of a taxpayer's property, including homes, vehicles, and land. It also attaches to all of your rights to other property, such as promissory notes or accounts receivable, and property acquired after the lien is filed. Essentially, anything of value can be included in the tax lien to satisfy the debt.

The IRS will issue a Release of the Notice of Federal Tax Lien under the following criteria:

- Within thirty days after a taxpayer satisfies his or her tax liabilities (including interest and penalties) by paying the debt or having it adjusted.
- Within thirty days after the IRS accepts a bond submitted by the taxpayer; the bond guarantees payment of the debt.
- The taxpayer must pay all fees that a state or other jurisdiction charges to file and release the IRS tax lien. The fees are added to the total amount owed.

The semi-good news is that a tax lien is usually released ten years after a tax is assessed. This is because ten years after the date of assessment, the ability for the IRS to collect the tax lapses. An IRS debt has a statute of limitations. And if the IRS negligently or knowingly fails to release your lien as required, you may sue the federal government for damages. People say you can't sue the government, but you can if this happens to you!

The Nitty-Gritty

Here are some things you should know if the IRS tries to file a tax lien against your home:

- By law, the IRS must notify you in writing not more than five business days after it files a tax lien.
- The IRS may notify you in person, by leaving the notice at your home or place of business, or by sending it via certified or registered mail to your last known address.
- You are entitled to ask an IRS manager to review your case and you may request a Collection Due Process hearing with the Office of Appeals by following the directions on the notice, but you must file this by the date specified.
- During the Collection Due Process hearing, you may dispute any information that is incorrect. For example, if you have proof that you paid all of the back taxes before the IRS filed the tax lien, now is the time to mention that.
- If the IRS filed the tax lien when you were in bankruptcy, you would be eligible for an automatic stay during bankruptcy proceedings.
- There is a statute of limitations, which is the time that the IRS has to collect the tax. If that expires before the IRS files the tax lien, you may be able to get the lien removed.

- If the IRS made a procedural error in their assessment of your tax debt, you are entitled to dispute that.
- If you were not given an opportunity to dispute the assessed tax liability, you may be able to provide documentation that will get the amount of the tax lien reduced.
- You are entitled to discuss your collection options during the review of your case.
- You are entitled to make spousal defenses that may affect the amount of your tax lien.

Lien and Mean

Here's a section from the IRS playbook that spells out what can be taken and for how long the lien remains in effect:

Internal Revenue Code Sec. 6321: Lien for Taxes

If any person liable to pay any tax neglects or refuses to pay the same after demand, the amount (including any interest, additional amount, addition to tax, or assessable penalty, together with any costs that may accrue in addition thereto) shall be a lien in favor of the United States upon all property and rights to property, whether real or personal, belonging to such person.

Internal Revenue Code Sec. 6322: Period of Lien

Unless another date is specifically fixed by law, the lien imposed by section 6321 shall arise at the time the assessment is made and shall continue until the liability for the amount so assessed (or a judgment against the taxpayer arising out of such liability) is satisfied or becomes unenforceable by reason of lapse of time.

The statute of limitations under which a federal tax lien may become "unenforceable by reason of lapse of time" is found at 26 U.S.C. § 6502. For taxes assessed on or after November 6, 1990, the lien generally becomes unenforceable ten years after the date of assessment. For taxes assessed on or before November 5,

1990, a prior version of section 6502 provides for a limitations period of six years after the date of assessment. Various exceptions may extend the time periods.

How to Get Rid of a Tax Lien

The situation may sound grim, but you can get yourself out from under a tax lien. The IRS will only release a lien when the debt is satisfied or the debt expires. The easiest way to do this is to pay your tax debt off immediately. Once the debt is paid, you need to obtain a Release of Federal Tax Lien. Once you request that your lien be removed, the IRS should remove the lien within thirty days and you will receive a Certificate of Release of Federal Tax Lien (Form 668Z).

To remove the lien from your home's title, you'll need to take your Certificate of Release to your local county recorder's office and pay a fee to have the certificate recorded. Once that is completed, you should send copies of the Certificate to each of the credit reporting agencies—TransUnion, Equifax, and Experian—so they can update your credit report and verify that the debt was paid. Unfortunately, the lien will still show up on your credit report for up to ten years, but at least the release of the lien will also be included as long as you notify the credit bureaus.

Some other common ways to stop tax liens on your home include:

- **Through an IRS Tax Lien Discharge or IRS Tax Lien Subordination**
  I already mentioned that the IRS may choose to subordinate or discharge a lien if the move will allow you to pay the agency more or pay the debt off sooner. Again, the decision is based on what is in the best interest of the IRS. If your home has equity, for example, you may be able to refinance your mortgage and free up enough cash to pay off your tax

bill. Or, you might consider selling your house, which could eliminate a hefty mortgage payment, thus increasing your ability to make monthly Installment Agreement payments. This can be a tough case to present to the IRS, so I would recommend you get help from a qualified tax professional before you approach the agency.

- **Negotiate a Settlement**
  Make a settlement with the IRS and then pay the settlement. Sounds simple, but the IRS does not engage in *Let's Make a Deal*. Instead, it has a handful of settlement programs, which I will fully describe in chapter 9. Find a solution that makes sense for your financial situation, pay off your debts as quickly as you can, and get the lien released.

- **Wait It Out**
  As mentioned previously, the ability for the IRS to collect tax debts does expire. This is called the Collection Statute Expiration Date. The vast majority of the time, this date comes to pass ten years after the tax is assessed. Once the ability for the IRS to collect expires, your debt practically expires, and your lien should self-release. You must be careful, though. The law provides the IRS a number of ways to extend the expiration date. And a lot of damage can be done to your credit in ten years, so I would not recommend this as a viable strategy for most people.

Other Options in a Nutshell

- **Beg, Borrow, or Steal**—Okay, well, scratch the steal part, but if you can swing it, you may be better off begging a family member or close friend to loan you the money so you can pay your back taxes. If your pride won't allow that, then consider borrowing the money from a credit card or home equity loan or even selling off that boat you only use twice a year. Sometimes, you just have to be a grown-up, buck up, and face facts: you are better off paying your taxes than losing everything you've got by trying to avoid the problem.

- **Partial Discharge**—This option may be at your disposal if you own a number of assets that have been included in your tax lien. That boat, for example, can be used to settle your IRS tax debt. You'll need to apply for what's called an "Application for Subordination of Federal Tax Lien" (Publication 784) and ask for a discharge. The IRS will determine the value of the asset and whether or not it satisfies your tax debt before it grants you this type of discharge.

- **Hardship**—It may be possible to prove to the IRS preemptively that you have absolutely no means by which to pay your tax debt. In this case, you may be granted hardship status and most likely your case will be classified as Currently Not Collectible, which I will fully explain in chapter 9. That still leaves you subject to collection at some point in the future, should your financial situation change, so it's best to consult with a qualified tax attorney to determine if this option is a possibility for you. And this option is really only effective if the IRS has not yet issued a lien. If the lien is already in place, being placed into Currently Not Collectible typically does not lead to the lien being released. Darn!

- **Bankruptcy**—Ehh, wrong answer! Do not under any circumstances let Fred, your well-meaning neighbor, or your cousin Vinnie convince you that your tax problems will magically disappear once you file for bankruptcy. Discharging taxes through bankruptcy, although possible, is much more difficult than for other forms of debt. So, if you are considering bankruptcy, I strongly encourage you to consult with a qualified attorney to help you determine if this is the right course of action for you to take.

- **Avoid Responsibility**—Ehh, wrong answer, again! Although I mentioned earlier there is a statute of limitations that the IRS follows for collecting tax debt—normally ten years—it is not a good idea to shirk your responsibility for ten years and hope that the IRS will forget about you. Trust me; it is not too busy to track you down. If you make no effort to work out your tax debt with the IRS, it can take your assets by force and you really want to avoid that, if possible. It may also use one of the other many weapons in its arsenal (levies, garnishments) to get your attention. Of course, if you have no assets, you may think you have nothing to lose. Think again! The tax lien and the fact that you never attempted to pay off the tax debt may stay on your credit record indefinitely.

Unfair? Incompetent? Never!

So what if you think the IRS is unfairly targeting you?

Let's say you paid your taxes late, but the IRS never updated your account. Or a glitch in the system credited your payment to another John Smith. Believe me; the IRS makes mistakes, so it's critical that you keep accurate records of your payments in case you need to defend yourself.

If the IRS files a tax lien against you when you know your tax bill is fully paid, under the "Taxpayer's Bill of Rights" you are entitled to a "Certificate of Release." The release should clearly state that the lien was filed in error. Once you have this document, you need to send copies to all three credit bureaus to minimize any ill effects the IRS error may have on your credit rating.

Impact of Foreclosures

There's no doubt about it, good people are losing their homes at a rapid rate. And if you owe back taxes, you're more likely to end up in foreclosure. Why? Well, the money you're paying out to the IRS is less money available to cover your mortgage.

According to CNN Money, U.S. government figures show a record three million households were hit with foreclosure in 2009. RealtyTrac, the online marketer of foreclosed homes, reported that one in forty-five households—or 2,824,674 properties nationwide—were in default last year.

That's 21 percent more than in 2008, and more than double 2007's total.

Foreclosure has a devastating emotional and financial impact on the poor family being forced out of their home. Beyond that, foreclosures have a ripple effect that goes way beyond hurting the homeowner—or even the mortgage lender. Foreclosures also invariably affect the entire neighboring community and can drastically impact local tax revenue.

Let's examine how that happens:

- **Decreasing Real Estate Values**—How do foreclosed homes diminish real estate values? In many ways, it's all under the radar. Although many foreclosures happen quietly and quickly, where neighbors don't even realize the house is empty until the foreclosure sale sign is in the yard, other homes are littered with huge warning signs, or sit on the market unkempt for months. Because no one is usually in charge of maintaining foreclosed homes, yards grow tall, pools fog up, and the whole home itself begins to look abandoned and prematurely aged. The property may begin to be occupied by squatters or even wildlife. In order to unload these properties, the banks will drastically reduce their asking price.

This forces regular sellers to lower their prices in order to stay competitive, which results in deflated real estate values for an entire neighborhood.

- **Devalued Neighborhoods**—In addition to forcing sellers to reduce prices, foreclosed homes can devalue a neighborhood just by sitting there unsold. As I mentioned before, the banks do not assign someone to look over the property, and if several homes on one street go into foreclosure, a once-friendly neighborhood can turn into a ghost town. Alternatively, it can become filled with drifters and squatters who do not value the property or location and may even bring more unsavory elements (e.g., drugs, crime, etc.) to the neighborhood. Once the area begins to decline, real estate values drop quickly, and residents will find it nearly impossible to sell their homes.

- **Loss of Local Revenue**—When a house has been vacated due to foreclosure, it means that there is no one living in the property, and there is no one to pay property taxes. This can be disastrous to local government agencies that rely on this revenue. For example, the municipality of Greenville, California, received more than 40 percent of its revenue from property taxes. In the past year alone, home values have decreased by more than 15 percent due to record foreclosure rates. This has led to a budget shortfall, leaving the town desperately struggling to get by. Other municipalities have even gone so far as to file for bankruptcy protection.

- **Reassessed Property Tax Rates**—Even if a foreclosed property is sold, the local government is going to get less money than it would have if the original homeowner had stayed. This is because property taxes are based on the value of the property, and if a house sells for significantly less than it did five years ago, then its tax rate will be reassessed and the tax-payer will only be required to pay the reduced property tax.

- **Additional Costs to Local Governments**—In addition to the lack of property tax revenue, the overall cost of a fore-closed home can be quite large. According to a study from Chicago, the cost of securing and processing a foreclosure can be as high as $5,400 per property. Furthermore, if the property is abandoned for more than a few months, local governments will lose out on utility taxes, and may have to pay for water service and trash removal. The total estimated cost on a foreclosed property could be as high as $20,000.

- **Local Service Cuts**—Without this valuable revenue from property taxes, many cities are trying to make up the revenue elsewhere. Local governments are being forced to lay off city workers (including firefighters and law enforcement officers), cut funding for education, increase retail taxes, and even sell precious historical landmarks. All this serves to drive good people and good business to greener pastures, perpetuating the problem.

The Alarming Rate of U.S. Home Foreclosures

According to Total Bankruptcy Inc., foreclosure rates in the United States are spreading like wildfire. A foreclosure action is taken *every ten seconds*. There were 1,528,364 total foreclosure actions taken in the first half of 2009. Home foreclosure also contributes to the over-all instability of the average American family.

Adding insult to injury, in the past, foreclosing on your mortgage would land you with a huge tax bill. Any portion of the debt that was forgiven or cancelled was taxed as income. Luckily, the government has made allowances in certain circumstances for debt forgiven on your primary residence.

New Rules on Dealing with Liens and Foreclosures

When the tsunami of foreclosures reached its peak at the turn of 2008–2009, the federal government was forced to step in and help millions of Americans facing the loss of their homes—or those who can't sell because of a tax lien on their house.

In a January 2009 media statement, the IRS announced an "expedited process that will make it easier for financially distressed homeowners to avoid having a federal tax lien block refinancing of mortgages or the sale of a home."

Loosely translated, that simply means if taxpayers are looking to refinance or sell a home and there is a federal tax lien filed, they do have options. According to the new IRS rules, taxpayers or their representatives, such as their lenders, may request that the IRS make a tax lien secondary to the lender's lien, allowing the owner to refinance or restructure a loan. Taxpayers or their representatives may also request that the IRS discharge its claim if the home is being sold for less than the amount of the mortgage lien under certain circumstances.

Under these new rules, getting a lien released is reportedly going to take less time—but don't hold your breath. The current process to request a discharge or a subordination of a tax lien takes

---

Tax Lady Tip

Foreclosure? No Deductions

The IRS takes a dim view of taxpayers trying to claim a loss on foreclosed property. The short and sweet story is that losses from the sale or foreclosure are not deductible. In fact, losses that end up being forgiven by the underlying mortgage holder may even be taxable!

approximately thirty days once the completed application is submitted. The IRS claims it will work to speed those requests in the wake of the economic downturn. When that increased speed of processing will begin is anyone's guess.

Having talked to an army of anxious, scared Americans who just found out they had a lien on their home for back taxes or were threatened with a lien, I have to say their number one concern—and that's a mild word when you're looking at someone who is literally at the edge of panic because of threats from the IRS—is that they will lose their home over back taxes.

Yep, I hear you. Is nothing sacred? Do these guys have to get their greedy mitts on *everything?*

Mortgage Forgiveness Debt Relief Act

According to the IRS website:

> The Mortgage Forgiveness Debt Relief Act of 2007 (updated in Dec. 2008) allows taxpayers to exclude income from the discharge of debt on their principal residence. Debt reduced through mortgage restructuring, as well as mortgage debt forgiven in connection with a foreclosure, qualifies for this relief.
>
> This provision applies to debt forgiven in calendar years 2007 through 2012. Up to $2 million of forgiven debt is eligible for this exclusion ($1 million if married and filing separately). The exclusion doesn't apply if the discharge is due to services performed for the lender or any other reason not directly related to a decline in the home's value or the taxpayer's financial condition. The amount excluded reduces the taxpayer's cost basis in the home.

When a Foreclosure Results in a Taxable Gain

Foreclosures are triggered when a bank or other mortgage lender repossesses a borrower's property and then sets about selling the property to satisfy the debt. By and large, a foreclosure occurs when the property's mortgage debt exceeds the property's fair market value. Under these conditions, the IRS views the foreclosure as a sale for the fair market value amount.

A tax gain will result if the property's fair market value exceeds its tax basis. According to IRS rules, the tax basis of a principal residence usually equals the original cost of the property, plus the cost of any improvements. On the other hand, a tax loss occurs if the property's fair market value is less than the tax basis.

In order to avoid a tax gain in a foreclosure, you should find out if you qualify for the federal home sale gain exclusion break. That break allows an unmarried person to pay no tax on a gain of up to $250,000, although married joint filers can exclude up to a $500,000 gain. To qualify, you must meet two conditions:

1. You owned the home for at least two years during the five-year period ending on the foreclosure date, and
2. You used the home as your principal residence for at least two years during the five-year period ending on that date.

Tax Gains and Foreclosures

The June 24, 2009, edition of *Smart Money* lays out some very useful examples of foreclosed principal residence scenarios to illustrate how the tax rules work.

Foreclosure with Tax Gain: Here's how a foreclosure scenario works out with tax gains.

Example: Say your home is foreclosed when its FMV is $325,000 and its tax basis is $275,000. There's a $250,000 first mortgage and a second of $180,000. So the total debt equals $430,000.

Assume the entire $250,000 first mortgage and $75,000 of the second get paid off when the lenders sell the property. That leaves an unpaid balance of $105,000 ($430,000 minus $325,000). You scrape together $25,000 to pay the balance down to $80,000, and the second mortgage lender forgives the rest.

Here are the tax results:

- The foreclosure triggers a $50,000 tax gain ($325,000 FMV minus $275,000 basis = $50,000 gain). For federal income tax purposes, you can probably exclude (pay no tax on) the gain thanks to the home sale gain exclusion break. (State income tax results may vary.)
- The $80,000 forgiven by the second mortgage lender is Cancellation of Debt (COD) income. It's taxable unless an exception applies.

Foreclosure with Tax Loss: It's also quite possible to have a principal residence foreclosure where the FMV of the property is less than its tax basis. In that case, you'll have a tax loss instead of a gain.

Example: Say the FMV of your principal residence is $300,000 when it's foreclosed, and the property's tax basis is $390,000. There's a $250,000 first mortgage and a second of $175,000, for total debt of $425,000.

The full $250,000 first mortgage and $50,000 of the second get paid off when the lenders sell the property. That leaves an unpaid balance of $125,000 ($425,000 minus $300,000). You scrape up enough to pay the balance down to $60,000, and the second mortgage lender forgives the rest.

The tax results are as follow:

- The foreclosure triggers a $90,000 tax loss ($300,000 FMV minus $390,000 basis = $90,000 loss). Unfortunately, the loss is considered a nondeductible personal expense for federal income tax purposes (and usually for state income tax purposes, too).
- The $60,000 forgiven by the second mortgage lender is COD income. It's taxable unless an exception applies. Once again, exceptions may apply.

Source: Smart Money, June 24, 2009, edition

Tax Implications of Multi-Generational Living

You ask, what is *multi-generational living*? If you live in a home with your children and your parents, you have a multi-generational household. In light of the struggling economy, some families are choosing to live in multi-generational households. Elderly parents are moving in with their adult children and so-called "boomerang" children are moving back in with their parents after college.

The sad truth is that foreclosures and tax liens not only affect the intended taxpayer but anyone else being supported by the taxpayer and living in the taxpayer's home. I can tell you that the fact that the downturn of the economy has driven many people to cut costs by moving in with family members does not faze the IRS or slow its collection efforts. It is relentless and will carry out the goal of collecting as much money from you as possible, no matter who is harmed in the process. The IRS says: too bad you need your hard-earned wages to help support your parents because they lost their home and moved in with you; forget about providing food for the family; if you can't pay now—we'll take your home.

Roni's Words of Wisdom

Going after your home is Exhibit A in the case against the IRS's "take no prisoners" mindset. I mean, for the love of God, these people will take your house and toss you out into the street and won't think twice about it.

So take tax liens seriously—because the IRS definitely will.

5

Work Release: Lose Your Job Without Losing Your Mind

It's a recession when your neighbor loses his job; it's a depression when you lose yours.

—HARRY S. TRUMAN

L osing a job in an economy where jobs just don't seem to exist is a shock to the system. The sad news is that the unemployment problem in the United States is actually far worse than you might think.

The U.S. government claims that only about 9.3 percent of Americans are out of work, but I know better. The numbers that the government uses come from a formula concocted by the Department of Labor's Bureau of Labor Statistics. But the formula is flawed, and so are the job numbers that scream from the headlines every month. The real unemployment number is 15 percent.

The criteria that the government uses doesn't account for people who have settled for part-time work, are sole proprietors without work, or who have simply stopped looking for work. That's right. It would appear that according to the government, people who have lost hope just don't count!

According to the Bureau of Labor Statistics (BLS), the government actually issues six jobless numbers (they're called *U1* through *U6*). The lowest is the number of workers unemployed for fifteen weeks or more and still looking for work, and the highest includes both the discouraged workers and part-time workers who want full-time jobs. The commonly quoted number you see on your favorite business news site or TV news broadcast is the U3, a rather optimistic compromise.

Houston, we have a problem. All of these numbers involve judgments about who is in and out of the labor force. But here's another group of numbers, also from the BLS, that perhaps gives a better picture.

The Real U.S. Jobs Numbers: As of March 2010

Total Employable: 237.159 million
Total Working: 138.905 million
Total Idle: 98.254 million

Percentage Idle to Total Employable: 40.5 percent (i.e., percent of Americans not working)

Total Working Full Time: 111.472 million
Total Working Part Time: 27.433 million
Total Not Working Full Time: 126.678 million
Total Searching for Work (the "Unemployed"): 15.005 million
Percentage "Unemployed" to Total Idle: 15.3 percent
Source: U.S. Bureau of Labor Statistics

Enlightening, isn't it? Realistically, the U.S. unemployment number was 15.4 percent at a time (in late 2009) when the federal government—and the lapdog media—were telling Americans it was just 9.7 percent as of March 2010.

Thus, my point is that dealing with a job loss is a lot more difficult—but a lot more common—than the government would have you believe. This glossing over of how bad it *really* is aggravates me to no end.

And can we talk about the way Americans get laid off? It's downright cruel. While researching this chapter, I read about a nurse in Wisconsin who was pulled out of surgery to be told she would be losing her job. Apparently, clinic officials were ordered by the parent company to fire ninety staff members immediately. One of the managers took that order quite literally.

Or how about this sick scheme? A large office campus was evacuated when the fire alarm rang. Hundreds of staffers were hustled out of the buildings. The employees gathered in groups in their assigned area, waiting for the signal to return to work, just like they had during every other fire drill. But that's not what happened. The manager in charge of the drill actually held several people back, saying it was a good time to tell them that they were being laid off. In fact, their security cards had already been deactivated and wouldn't let them back in the building.

These issues really hit home to me—especially when you throw a big tax debt into the mix. As the child of a single mother, I learned quickly how important a job really is to a family. Growing up as an American who loves her country, I also knew that paying taxes was a by-product of having that job. And that's not such a bad thing. After all, if you're paying taxes, it means you have a job and you're making money. And merely having a job is definitely a good thing!

So although I've made a career—make that a passion—out of battling the IRS over taxes on behalf of average Americans, I know that paying taxes is also part of living in a civil society.

You know what they say: if you want to have a dance, you've got to pay the band. But sometimes life knocks you on your rear end and you can't afford to pay your taxes. That's exactly what happens to a lot of people who lose their jobs. It's a pretty common occurrence these days.

What to Do if Your Employment Situation Collapses

Uh-oh. You know those rumors running rampant throughout the office the last few weeks, the ones that whispered *cutbacks* and *lay-offs*? Unfortunately for you, they're true. And your job could be cut next.

Don't feel too bad. Your misery has a lot of company. According to the International Labor Organization (ILO), approximately twenty million jobs have been lost in the United States through 2009 due to the crisis—mostly in construction, real estate, financial services, and the auto sector—bringing world unemployment well above two hundred million for the first time ever. The number of unemployed people worldwide could increase by an additional fifty million in 2010 as the global recession intensifies, as forecast by the ILO.

Yet even though it's a tough time emotionally, the importance of keeping a cool head cannot be underestimated. There's a lot at stake

Unemployment Blues

These states have unemployment rates that are higher than the national average (as of January 2010):

Michigan	14.1	Ohio	11
Nevada	13.4	North Carolina	11.1
Rhode Island	12.6	Tennessee	11.6
California	12.6	Florida	12.3
Oregon	10.6	Alabama	11
South Carolina	12.2	Georgia	10.6
District of Columbia	11.6	Illinois	11.5
Kentucky	10.7	Indiana	9.9

Source: Bureau of Labor Statistics

here, like getting everything you can from your benefits and making the right moves with your retirement plan.

Job one is to handle your severance package—if you get one. Severance is supposed to fill the income gap until you find a new gig. Most severance packages are based on years of service to the company. Unfortunately, this formula ignores the fact that the biggest factors in the length of time between jobs are your age and your salary level. The older you are and the more you made, the longer your employment gap tends to be. Seems pretty unfair, doesn't it? I completely agree, but until corporate America starts doing right by its employees, we have to work with what we've got. This means getting an average of one or two weeks' pay per year of service.

I would advise that you hold off on signing your severance agreement until you have had time to read it fully, think it over, and do a little research to ensure you're getting a decent deal. You can always hire an attorney to review the agreement to make absolutely sure you aren't getting a bum deal, but it usually isn't necessary.

It is also critical to document everything. Save your emails, memos, contracts, awards, and promotions, along with any employee manuals. You never know when you'll need to protect yourself, and having the information ready at hand is the best way to do that.

Some Commonsense Tips

- **Keep severance pay in a liquid account**—Your best bet is a money market or savings account. That way, you can get your hands on the money if you need it quickly, but you still get a higher interest rate than keeping it in your checking account.
- **Take a lump sum**—If you are given the choice of taking severance in a lump sum or in periodic payments, it's usually better to opt for a lump sum so you can invest the money and start earning interest right away. If you sense that your

old firm is in financial jeopardy, the decision is a no-brainer: take the money.

- **Outplacement**—Approximately 80 percent of employers in the United States provide outplacement services to laid-off employees. Ask if your former company does.
- **Vacation Pay**—If a company allows its employees to accrue vacation time from one year to the next, employees who have been laid off should remember to account for their unused vacation time.
- **Stock Options**—Generally, departing employees have 90 days after they've been laid off to exercise vested stock options before the options are lost. Sometimes employees can negotiate to have this period extended and even have unvested options become exercisable.
- **Non-Compete Agreements**—Non-compete agreements disallow employees from working for a company in the same field or providing the same products and services as their former employer. If you are asked to sign one of these, don't sign until you talk to a lawyer. If you must sign such an agreement or you are dealing with the aftermath of an agreement you previously signed, check for time limits (non-competes don't go on forever), find out whether or not you're eligible

When in Doubt Fill It Out

You still have W-2 obligations, even if you're out of a job. The IRS is clear on who needs to file taxes. By law, Uncle Sam insists anyone who gets a W-2 from his or her employer and earned at least $8,950 (if you're single and younger than sixty-five years old) or earned at least $400 from self-employment income must file a tax return. So, even if you are not working right now, you still may need to file at tax return.

to "compete" with your ex-company in a different state or country, and be certain which industries you're barred from working in or under what limits you're operating. I know it's expensive (probably a few hundred dollars), but having a good attorney review your non-compete agreement can save you a lot of trouble.

- **Medical Insurance**—Employers with more than twenty employees must, according to law, offer employees Consolidated Omnibus Reconciliation Act (COBRA) coverage for eighteen months after they leave the organization. COBRA allows you to spend up to eighteen months on your former employer's health plan—but you will usually have to pay the entire cost of the insurance. You also usually have a waiting period before COBRA kicks in, but most employers will continue your coverage in the interim. If your spouse has medical coverage through his or her employer, you may be better off switching to that plan.

- **Cash In on Your Spending Plan**—If you've been contributing pretax money from your wages to a flexible spending account to cover unreimbursed medical bills, make an appointment to talk with your benefits officer. Any money left in this plan at the end of the year goes to the employer, not to you. Hard to believe but true! This is informally known as the "use it or lose it" rule. Find out how your company handles the situation when employees are let go. You can use the funds to stock up on contact lenses, prescription glasses, prescription drugs, hearing aids, or go ahead and get that physical you've been putting off.

- **Move Your 401(k)**—Some 401(k) retirement plans let you leave your money invested when you go. Some even continue to match contributions for a period of time. Most, however, want you off the books pronto. In that case, you need a temporary solution. I recommend parking your funds in an

IRA. You can eventually roll the funds over to a new plan. Just make sure the plan administrator is the one making the transactions. If you withdraw the funds, even just to place them in another retirement plan, 20 percent will automatically be withheld for taxes. Avoid the hassle, and have the transactions completed by plan administrators.

If You're Laid Off, Call the IRS

If you get laid off and believe you'll have trouble paying your tax bill, contact the IRS right away. Call the IRS at 1-800-829-1040 if you lost your job, had a reduction in income, or cannot pay your taxes. By being proactive, you increase the chances of being granted a waiver or negotiating an Installment Agreement. You are always better off getting in front of the problem than hiding out and hoping the IRS won't notice you.

The Tax Ramifications of Losing Your Job

Losing your job is stressful. Let's face it, it just plain sucks. And the IRS is not going out of its way to make it any easier. But no matter how aggravating the experience can be, you still have to take care of business tax-wise.

Unemployment benefits are a godsend for those facing a job loss. And, up until very recently, Congress has been aggressive about extending those benefits as layoffs continue and new jobs are harder to come by. Here's the issue: unemployment aid has quickly become a huge expense in the federal budget—an estimated $200 billion to be paid out this year. So the bad news is that Congress is now heavily considering limiting how many weeks one may receive aid to only ninety-nine weeks. In the coming months, over one million Americans will be unemployed and ineligible to continue to receive unemployment aid.

So, if you are lucky enough to receive unemployment assistance, keep in mind that you will have to pay taxes on these funds, and withholding is not automatic. This can result in some hefty tax debts for people already struggling to make ends meet after losing their jobs. Here are some helpful tips and action steps to help you avoid a nasty tax debt:

Taxable Income: Make no mistake, the money you receive from unemployment benefits is taxable income. Some people are so relieved to have an income they overlook the tax consequences. This means that you are going to owe both federal and state income taxes on it (if your state has an income tax).

> *Action Step:* Your best bet to avoid a surprise tax bill while you're unemployed is to have taxes withheld from your unemployment payments. Aim for 10 percent withheld for federal taxes; however, you will have to check your state's rules to determine how much you will need to withhold for state tax purposes. You can do this when you apply for unemployment or you can complete Form W-4V Voluntary Withholding Request and submit it to your unemployment office. Just make sure you take a close look at your unemployment checks to make sure taxes are actually being withheld. Hey, mistakes happen, and you'll be the one left paying for them if you aren't careful.

The First $2,400 is Tax-Free: Starting in 2009, you don't have to pay taxes on the first $2,400 in unemployment benefits you receive. The $2,400 tax break was part of the new 2009 American Recovery and Reinvestment Act and so only affected the 2009 tax year. All benefits from the year 2008 and before are fully taxable. Sure, Congress may extend the tax break, but then again, it might not.

> *Action Step:* Make sure you subtract $2,400 from your total unemployment benefits before you report it on your tax return.

Severance Pay: Getting severance pay? Good for you. Anything you can get out of those bloodsuckers who laid you off is okay by me. Just remember that any severance you receive is also considered taxable income. This includes any one-time payments, as well as payouts for accumulated vacation or sick leave benefits. It's all taxed as ordinary income.

> *Action Step:* Take a close look at your severance payments to see if taxes were withheld. If not, you may need to increase your other tax withholdings to avoid a tax bill. Then, make sure you report all severance on your tax returns.

Estimated Payments: Quarterly payments may help protect you against any big tax liability. If, for any reason, you do not choose to have taxes withheld on your unemployment, you should consider making an estimated quarterly payment. It takes some discipline to pay estimated taxes four times a year, but it beats getting hit with an underpayment penalty at tax time.

> *Action Step:* Work with a professional tax advisor to determine how much you should be paying the IRS. Then set up your regular payments. I recommend using the IRS's online Electronic Federal Tax Payment System (EFTPS). It's provided free of charge by the U.S. Department of Treasury. It's faster, safer, and much more convenient than mailing in a paper check.

State Taxes: What? You thought that your state wouldn't come knocking for its share of your unemployment benefits? Silly you! If your state has an income tax, then you will probably have to pay income taxes on your unemployment benefits.

> *Action Step:* Every state is different, so before making any decisions, check with your state's revenue department (find contact information for all fifty states' departments in chapter 12) or ask a tax professional for help.

Job Hunt: They say that looking for a full-time job is, well, a full-time job. One silver lining—besides eventually landing a good job—is that job-hunting expenses are tax deductible. That includes placement agency costs, printing resumes, fax and phone expenses, mileage, and the list goes on. Check for similar deductions for your state as well.

> *Action Step:* Log all job-search-related fees and expenses, including mileage, employment agency fees, supplies, mailing expenses, phone calls, Internet job site fees, and career-related coaching. If you don't log it, you'll have a hard time remembering it all or proving it all should the IRS decide to take a closer look.

Straight from the Horse's Mouth: What the IRS Says about Unemployment and Your Taxes

In a nutshell, here is what the IRS has to say about losing your job:

- Unemployment compensation is taxable income, so be sure to have taxes withheld or make estimated payments so you don't owe money come tax time.
- For 2009, the first $2,400 of unemployment wages do not have to be included in your gross income.
- Severance pay is taxable income in the year that it is received.
- Extended unemployment benefits (thirteen weeks extra) are taxable.
- Final payments for vacation or sick leave from your employer are taxable; usually your employer will deduct the taxes for you.
- Public assistance and food stamps are not taxable income.

Source: Tax Impact of Job Loss; Publication 4128 (Rev. 8-2008)

Going the Freelance Route? Be Prepared

If you strike out on your own after a job loss, that has tax ramifications, too.

For example, many people use their time unemployed to do some freelance work. This can be a great way to bring in some cash. And many a small business was started just like this. Just remember, anything you earn is considered self-employment income. That means you are responsible for not just income tax but also self-employment tax. Yes, on top of your normal income taxes, you need to be paying 15.3 percent of your net profit to cover your Social Security and Medicare taxes.

- If you earned more than $400 from your freelance work, you need to file a tax return and a Schedule C showing your income and expenses.
- If you earned more than $600 from one project, you should receive Form 1099 from your client. This will detail how much you were paid, and any taxes paid out from your earnings.
- Whether you receive a 1099 or not, you must report all income to the IRS. Remember, it gets financial information from your clients and from your financial institutions, so it knows more than you think.

To make your taxes a little more complicated, you can be an employee and an employer in the same year. If you worked for someone else for part of the year, then did freelance work after getting laid off, you'll get a W-2 from your employer and 1099s from your freelance clients. If this sounds a little tricky, it can be. When in doubt, get the help of a qualified tax professional.

More Tax Tips for the Unemployed

Here are some additional ways to make the most of your taxes if you are one of the millions currently struggling with unemployment:

- **Charity ends at home**—If you received public assistance, like food stamps or WIC, or if someone gave you money to help you out, those forms of income are not taxable.
- **Deal in deductions**—Because your income was cut off, you are probably going to have a lower adjusted gross income (AGI) than in years past. Thus, you may be able to deduct medical expenses, student loan interest, and other miscellaneous deductions that you weren't eligible to claim in the past. For example, you can usually only deduct medical expenses that exceed 7.5 percent of your AGI, which makes many employed people and those with employer-provided health care ineligible. However, with a lower AGI, more of these expenses will become deductible. Also, remember that if you are paying COBRA fees to keep your medical insurance, you can deduct those fees as well.
- **Get cash from your IRA**—You may be able to undo your IRA contributions from earlier in the year. This means you can withdraw the amount you put in without tax hits. The only trick here is that you cannot also claim a deduction for those contributions, and you must still include any income, like interest, you earned from the contribution.
- **Take stock**—This could be the perfect opportunity to dump some loser stocks and use capital losses to your advantage. Generally, capital losses locked in by selling stocks are used to negate capital gains. However, if you have no capital gains or have more losses than gains, you can use up to $3,000 of that loss to negate ordinary income. You can also carry the remainder of the loss forward into future years until you deplete the entire loss. And of course, one of the best parts is that by selling the stocks, you get an instant cash infusion.

What Not to Do: Cash-Out and Carry at Your Own Peril

One mistake some preoccupied people make when dealing with a job loss is to take out their 401(k) proceeds in the form of a cash distribution. Big mistake.

If you decide to withdraw your retirement money rather than leave it where it is or roll it over into an IRA, you risk losing up to half your investment in taxes and penalties, depending on your income tax bracket.

Right off the bat, Uncle Sam will peel 20 percent of your retirement plan proceeds away in the form of a federal income tax prepayment. And, if your tax bracket is higher than that 20 percent, you'll have to pay more come tax season—the difference between that 20 percent and your own income tax rate. For example, an investor in the 31 percent bracket who cashes out $100,000 from a 401(k) would have to make an automatic 20 percent prepayment to the IRS. And come tax time, he or she would have to fork over an additional 11 percent, for a total tax of 31 percent.

That's not all. If you're under fifty-five, the IRS will also stick you with an early withdrawal penalty, worth another 10 percent of your total distribution. Your home state may want a cut, too. Yikes!

The best move to make is to have your plan administrator roll over your 401(k) plan either into an IRA or into your new employer's 401(k) plan. That will help you avoid all the taxes and penalties of making a cash withdrawal and allows you to consolidate all your retirement funds in one place. The process usually involves filling out a form to transfer funds from your old employer and an application to choose among the funds available. The plan administrator for your new company will be glad to steer you through the rollover process. Your bank may also be a good source of expertise if you decide to roll your retirement funds over into an IRA.

In some cases, your old employer may allow you to leave your retirement funds in its 401(k) plan. It may make your skin crawl, but it's a much better option than taking your cash out directly.

I know a job loss is awful. Too many people panic and pull cash out of their retirement plans. Remember, you have other options, like unemployment and public assistance programs to help you get by. So think hard before you pull the plug on your retirement savings and end up with big tax problems.

Roni's Soapbox

Losing your job can be devastating. But losing your job does not excuse you from your tax obligations. We all enjoy the benefits of living in a civilized society, so we must all pay the price.

That said, losing your job is enough of a burden without having to face the IRS. The Internal Revenue Service is a soulless machine—cold, remorseless, and completely indifferent to the fact that you lost your job and are facing legitimate financial difficulties.

It's shameless but perfectly legal. If you wind up owing back taxes due to a job loss, the penalties for not being prepared can be severe and long lasting.

Even in this economy—no, especially in this economy—Congress and the White House need tax money. And they've tasked the IRS with collecting every dime it can. And with less money available for collecting, the IRS will not be merciful because you're having a tough time.

The reckoning is coming, so you'd better be ready.

6

You, Your Business, and the IRS— A Beautiful Partnership or a Messy Divorce

A corporation's primary goal is to make money. Government's primary role is to take a big chunk of that money and give it to others.

—LARRY ELLISON

I don't think there is anything more American than striking out on your own in the business world. We are a country full of entrepreneurs—creative people who are not satisfied to work themselves to death making someone else rich.

Small business is one of the biggest driving forces of the American economy. The Small Business Administration states that small businesses account for 99.7 percent of our country's employer businesses.

So, because small businesses are so crucial to our economic survival, the IRS must be kind and lenient with business owners, right?

Think again. What the IRS will do to a small business owner who makes a mistake on his or her taxes is enough to make you sick.

Take the case of carwash owner Orman Wilson. To help his employees a few years back, Wilson created a pension plan for himself and his staff.

No big deal, right?

But what happened next, as fully chronicled in the *Wall Street Journal*, is pretty typical of the sorry way that the U.S. government treats small business owners. The *Journal*'s article tells the story:

> Mr. Wilson, the owner of 19 coin-operated car washes in Houston, says he relied on four advisers, including a certified public accountant, to set up a plan that received approval from the Internal Revenue Service. Then, in late 2007, the IRS found fault with the plan and assessed it $250,000—plus special penalties of $1.2 million.
>
> The penalties "would wipe us out," Mr. Wilson says.
>
> Hundreds of small-business owners have been hit with similar penalties in connection with pension or benefit plans, says Alex Brucker of the Small Business Council of America, an association representing small firms on pension, tax and health-care issues. Hundreds more are likely to get hit with these penalties in the near future, he says.

The source of the distress: tax law changes made by Congress in 2004. At the time, lawmakers were worried that tax shelters, especially those used by large corporations, were costing the Treasury billions in revenue. To combat it, they imposed enormous fines on taxpayers who failed to inform the IRS of participation in any transaction the agency might consider a tax shelter.

True to form, the IRS screwed up royally on this one—and left Wilson holding the bag. As the *Journal* reported, the IRS fines weren't for any tax shelter but for not filing a tax form letting Uncle

Sam know about the transaction. One missing form was costing a well-meaning business owner his livelihood.

According to the IRS, the penalty that snared the small car wash owner is $100,000 per offense per year for individuals and $200,000 for businesses. Worse, there is no way for citizens like Wilson to get the penalties reviewed in Tax Court.

National Taxpayer Advocate Nina Olson told the *Journal* that the fines "have the effect of bankrupting middle class families who had no intention of entering into a tax shelter." In this case, it had the effect of running a good guy out of business and costing his employees their jobs.

Wilson's story is a prime example of the IRS lacking any sense or common decency and using tax laws to beat up on an innocent business owner.

Let me give you another example of how well the IRS treats business owners that owe a tax tab. Just recently, the story of a Sacramento car wash owner owing the IRS a mere $.04 made national news. The IRS showed up at the business CIA-style, in black cars and suits, to collect the $.04 tab. Ridiculous!

Owning your business is fantastic. I can't recommend it highly enough. However, one big potential downside of owning your own business is dealing with the IRS. The agency has a whole different set of rules and regulations for business owners. If you want to keep your business open and thriving, you'd better learn those rules and follow them to the letter—or face the full wrath of the IRS.

If your business gets into financial trouble or worse, goes under, don't expect much sympathy from the IRS. No, I daresay it will work even harder to get its cash from you while it still can. So, you must be prepared or the IRS will steamroll you in a heartbeat.

Let's make sure this doesn't happen to you. You need to pay particular attention to the key rules and strategies you'll need should you find yourself on the wrong end of a tax debt.

Let's have a look and see how high a wall and deep a moat we can build between your small business and the IRS.

Tax Implications of Starting Your Own Business

Once you've decided to hang out your shingle, so to speak, you're going to enter a whole new world of tax obligations.

To begin with, if you've worked as a wage-earning employee during the same year that you start your business, remember that you will need to report both your wages and your business income to the IRS. This means that you will likely have to file a few more forms with your tax return than usual.

In general, businesses are taxed on business income minus business expenses. Now, how those taxes are reported and paid will depend on how you set up your business. I'm talking about company structure here, and it makes a huge difference in how your taxes will work.

Small Business, Big Target

Be careful if you're a small business owner. According to IRS numbers, small business owners are the number one targets of tax audits. In fact, more than 40 percent of the agency's audit budget goes toward investigating small business owners. In addition, the Schedule C tax form, which small business owners use to report income, is the single most audited business form.

Types of Business Structures

Many people don't think too hard about how they will structure their fledgling company, and that's a shame. I think deciding the structure should be your second priority, right after you figure out what your company will make or sell.

Choosing the right structure for your business entity is important. The type of entity you create will have a long-reaching effect on how much control you have over company decisions, how much personal liability you have, and, of course, how you pay taxes for your business income.

There are two methods of taxing a business: corporate and pass-through. In a corporate structure, the company is a taxable entity in and of itself. In a pass-through structure, 100 percent of income taxes are reported and paid by the business owners.

Corporate Method

The following organizations are generally taxed under the corporate method:

- Standard C Corporations
- Non-Profit or Not-For-Profit Organizations
- LLCs in some circumstances

Corporations generally have the benefit of protecting shareholders from personal liability. In fact, the corporation is a completely separate and distinct legal entity. Once formed, the corporation essentially becomes a person in the eyes of the government, complete with a number of protections and obligations that come with it.

On the positive side, the shareholders are not held personally liable for corporate debts or lawsuits against the company and they can't lose assets to legal claims against the corporation. For tax purposes, this means that if the corporation incurs a tax debt, the IRS can only collect from the company and cannot come after the shareholders for any portion of the debt.

On the negative side of things, corporations are double taxed. All company profits are taxed at the corporate tax rates, and then the shareholders' dividends are taxed as income for each individual.

Corporations must prepare financial statements and tax returns for the company income and expenses. Corporations must generally pay estimated taxes throughout the year, with a full estimated tax report filed annually.

The company shareholders must then prepare their own tax returns reporting all income they receive from the company. You can see how corporations can end up flooded with paperwork.

Piercing the Corporate Veil

Generally speaking, corporations are treated as separate legal entities from company shareholders. However, in extreme circumstances, individual shareholders may be held liable for company actions. When a court decides to hold an individual shareholder accountable for actions or behaviors carried out by the company, it's called *piercing the corporate veil*.

This is a heavily debated issue in corporate legal circles, and no hard and fast rules determine when the corporate veil should be pierced. Often, it occurs when a court determines that the corporation was markedly noncompliant or if the shareholders used company funds as personal funds, for example.

If you decide to organize your business as a corporation, you can be both a shareholder and an employee of the corporation, receiving both dividends and a salary for your work. You might even be the only employee of your corporation, and that's OK. Just make sure you report both forms of income when you file your taxes and follow all payroll tax rules for yourself. We'll get into payroll taxes more later on.

Non-profit corporations are organizations that are not set up to make a profit. Rather, they exist to achieve a mission, such as feeding the hungry or ending child abuse. Although charitable organizations are the most obvious example, theater companies, civic organizations, and other artistic endeavors are often run by non-profits. Because these organizations are not in it for profit, they are exempt from paying federal or state income taxes.

Why would someone want to start a non-profit corporation? Remember, it's only the organization as a whole that cannot turn a profit. As an employee of the non-profit, you can earn a respectable salary. Because non-profits are tax-exempt organizations, the rules governing them are very strict. And not having to pay taxes does not mean you won't have to deal with the IRS. No, you still have to report income and expenses, and your organization's activities are closely monitored to avoid abuse of the tax-exempt status.

Tax Forms for Corporations

- Form 1120 U.S. Corporate Income Tax Return
- Form 1120-W Estimated Tax For Corporations
- 8109-B Federal Tax Deposit Coupon

Tax Forms for Non-Profit Corporations

- Form 1023 Application for Recognition of Exemption
- Form 990-N, 990-EZ, 990 Return of Organization Exempt from Income Tax

Pass-Through Method

The following organizations are generally taxed under the pass-through method:

- Sole Proprietors
- Partnerships
- S-Corporations
- Limited Liability Corporations (LLCs)—in some circumstances

Many small businesses start out as sole proprietorships. This is a fairly easy structure to set up with a minimal amount of bureaucracy involved. As a sole proprietor, you get to have control over how you run your business, and all the profits are yours. But along with the control comes the liability. If your business is sued or winds up with an IRS debt, your personal assets are fair game.

Tax Forms for Sole Proprietorships

- 1040 U.S. Individual Income Tax Return
- Schedule C Profit or Loss from Business
- Schedule SE Self-Employment Tax
- 1040 ES Estimated Tax for Individuals

The IRS views you and your business as one taxable entity. All business profits are reported on your personal income tax filings, and all profits are taxed at your personal tax rates. Because taxes will not automatically be withheld from your business income, you must make estimated tax payments on a quarterly or monthly basis.

You will also need to satisfy your Social Security and Medicare obligations by paying self-employment taxes, which add up to 15.3 percent of your business profits.

Partnerships are another common business structure for new entrepreneurs. Each partner may have a variety of responsibilities, depending on how you choose to structure the partnership. Like sole proprietors, you, as a partner, have complete control over decision-making and profits. Of course, along with this control comes liability, though depending on how you organize the partnership, financial liability may not be equally shared.

From a tax perspective, your partnership is not a separate tax entity. You will file an annual informational return (reporting all income, deductions, gains, losses, etc.) on behalf of the business, but all profits and losses are passed through to you and your partners and are reported on your respective tax returns.

As a partner, you are not an employee of the company. Therefore, the business must supply copies of Schedule K-1 (Form 1065 U.S. Return of Partnership Income) to you and your partners. You are responsible for reporting your share of income tax on Form 1040, and for paying all estimated taxes and all employment taxes, as discussed previously.

S corporations are a hybrid of corporations and partnerships. Like partnerships, the business income and expenses are passed through to the shareholders and taxed at each shareholder's individual

Tax Forms for Partnerships

- Form 1065 U.S. Return of Partnership Income
- Form 941 Employer's Quarterly Federal Tax Return
- Form 940 Employer's Annual Federal Unemployment Tax Return
- Form 8109-B Federal Tax Deposit Coupon
- Form 1040 U.S. Individual Income Tax Return
- Schedule E Supplemental Income and Loss
- Schedule SE Self-Employment Tax
- 1040 ES Estimated Tax For Individuals

tax rate. This means that shareholders report their share of the profits, losses, deductions, and credits on their personal tax returns.

On the other hand, like corporations, individual shareholders are not usually financially or legally liable for the company.

If you are a shareholder who performs any work for the company, you must be paid a salary in addition to any profits you receive. This will mean you will report income from your W-2 wages in addition to your shareholder profits. This should not be too difficult but will add a little complexity to your taxes.

From a tax perspective, S corporations must file an informational return reporting all income, deductions, and credits to the IRS using Form 1120S U.S. Income Tax Return for an S Corporation. The company may also need to make estimated payments for:

1. Tax on built-in gains;
2. Excess net passive income tax; and
3. Investment credit recapture tax.

Additionally, like all businesses, the S corporation must pay employment taxes, including Social Security, Medicare, and unemployment taxes.

Tax Forms for S Corporations

- Form 1120S U.S. Income Tax Return for an S Corporation
- Form 1120-W Estimated Tax for Corporations
- Form 941 Employer's Quarterly Federal Tax Return
- Form 940 Employer's Annual Federal Unemployment Tax Return
- Form 1040 U.S. Individual Income Tax Return
- Schedule E Supplemental Income and Loss
- 1040 ES Estimated Tax For Individuals

LLCs are an interesting breed of business structure. The IRS calls these "check the box" entities, meaning they can be taxed as either a corporate or a pass-through entity by the LLC shareholder's choice.

LLCs are chartered by individual states, thus each state may have different rules for forming, governing, and operating this business type. Generally, owners of an LLC are called members, and most states do not restrict membership, meaning an individual, a partnership, and even an entire corporation can be a member of an LLC. You may even have single-member LLCs, meaning only one person or company owns the company.

The LLC's members must elect how they will pay taxes on company profits. This is done using Form 9932 Entity Classification Election. Along with all the options in tax payment methods comes a lot of ambiguity for filing.

Tax Forms for LLCs

- Schedule C Profit or Loss from Business
- Schedule E Supplemental Income and Loss
- Schedule SE Self-Employment Tax
- Schedule ES Estimated Tax For Individuals
- W-2 Wage and Tax Statement
- Form 941 Employer's Quarterly Federal Tax Return
- Form 940 Employer's Annual Federal Unemployment Tax Return
- Form 944 Employer's Annual Federal Tax Return
- Form 1065 U.S. Return of Partnership Income
- Form 1096 Annual Summary and Transmittal of U.S. Information Returns
- Form 1120 U.S. Corporation Income Tax Return
- Form 1120-S U.S. Income Tax Return for an S Corporation
- Form 8832 Entity Classification Election

Choosing Your Entity

I've heard plenty of discussion among so-called business experts about exactly how you should structure your business. Some of it is useful, but most of the advice I've gotten was bull. Here's what I've learned:

Generally, you should incorporate in the state where you conduct business. If you do business in several states or all over the United States, then you should incorporate in the state where your headquarters will be located. And you may need to register your business in each state where you have an actual physical address.

But that's not the only way. Ever notice how a lot of companies are incorporated in Nevada and Delaware? That's because these two states have extremely proactive business laws and tax regulations. Depending upon your specific business and situation, you may find it beneficial to incorporate in a more business-friendly state. Just make sure you consult an attorney who specializes in business law to make sure everything is buttoned up.

Paying Taxes as a Business Owner

Business owners are taxed on the business income minus the business expenses. You are supposed to pay your taxes on a quarterly basis, using Form 1040ES Estimated Tax. Generally, you have to make these estimated tax payments if you expect to have a tax liability of more than $1,000 when you file your tax return.

If your income will be about the same as last year, pull out your last tax return, find how much you paid in taxes last year, and divide it by four. This is a simple way to estimate what your quarterly payment should be. Remember, though, that you must also pay Social Security and Medicare taxes, totaling an additional 15.3 percent of your total income.

In a nutshell, here are the biggest tax issues to consider for your business:

- I've mentioned this before, but it's worth mentioning again. Under the tax law, you can be both an employee and a business owner at the same time, if you choose. The primary issue is to report all income on your return.
- Make sure you fully understand how your business is supposed to report and pay taxes. This will depend upon how you structured your business.

Payroll Taxes

If you have any employees, you must pay payroll taxes. Federal payroll taxes are split between the employee and the employer. Each

Business Taxes You've Got to Pay

As a sole proprietor, at a minimum, you are responsible for:

- Self-Employment Tax
- Estimated Taxes

For other small business owners, all the taxes listed must be paid, plus a few more:

- Payroll Taxes (this includes deducting federal, state, and sometimes county and city income taxes from your employees' wages, in addition to Social Security and Medicare taxes.)
- Unemployment Taxes
- Property Taxes
- Heavy Highway Use Tax
- Excise Tax
- Sales Tax

contributes approximately 7.5 percent of the employee's wages to pay into the Social Security and Medicare programs. However, as an employer, you must collect all of the federal payroll tax—both the employer's portion and the employee's portion—and deposit these taxes as required by law.

In addition, you are on the hook for Federal Unemployment Taxes (FUTA). You pay this straight from your business funds; employees do not pay this tax. Use Form 941 Employer's Annual Federal Unemployment Tax Return.

Operational Issues

Once you have your business up and running, your focus, as far as keeping the IRS at bay, is to minimize potential problems with your tax obligations.

What are the odds of ever having trouble with the IRS? The truth is, your odds of having some kind of issue are actually pretty good. As you can see, there are a lot of obligations and rules surrounding businesses and taxes, and it's entirely too easy for busy owners to make a mistake somewhere along the line.

Here are some of the most common tax problems I see with small business owners and Uncle Sam:

- **Failure to Withhold Payroll Taxes**—For business owners, especially in their first year of business when the learning curve is especially steep, neglecting to withhold payroll taxes is a common problem. The penalty for this equals the amount of the taxes that are owed. Tax specialists call that the "100 Percent Payroll Penalty" or "Trust Fund Recovery Penalty" (TFRP). Once a TFRP is imposed, the employment taxes are held in a trust, basically as property of the U.S. government, until they are due to be paid.

What is the U.S. Federal Government Self-Employment Tax Rate?

In 2009, the self-employment tax rate was 15.3 percent (12.4 percent goes to fund Social Security and 2.9 percent is applied to Medicare).

Here's a breakdown:

Self-Employment Tax Rates			
Year	**2008**	**2009**	**2010**
Social Security	12.4 percent on self-employment income up to $102,000	12.4 percent on self-employment income up to $106,800	12.4 percent on self-employment income up to $106,800
Medicare	12.4 percent on self-employment income up to $102,000	Plus 2.9 percent for Medicare tax on earnings more than $106,800	Plus 2.9 percent for Medicare tax on earnings more than $106,800

Source: Social Security Administration. "Electronic Fact Sheet," January 21, 2010.

- **Categorizing Employees**—The IRS is big on labeling your staffers. The two most prominent classifications are *employees* and *independent contractors*. Many employers try to make their own lives easier by classifying all their workers as independent contractors. Here's the problem: if the IRS doesn't agree with that classification, it will call it theft of tax funds, and slam you with some nasty penalties. Form SS-8—Determination of Employee Work Status for Purposes of Federal Income Tax Withholding—will help you determine the important differences between an employee and an independent contractor.

Key Differences Between
Employees and Independent Contractors

Behavior Control	
Employee	**Independent Contractor**
Business directly controls how the work is done, the time in which it is done, and method	Worker is able to control the method and how the job will be completed and generally provides the estimated timeframe
Financial Control	
Employee	**Independent Contractor**
Business has the right to direct or control the financial and business aspects of the worker's job, including:	The worker has the right to direct and control all financial and business aspects of the job, including:
• The extent to which the worker has unreimbursed business expenses;	• The extent to which the worker has unreimbursed business expenses;
• The extent of the worker's investment in the facilities used in performing services;	• The extent of the worker's investment in the facilities used in performing services;
• The extent to which the worker makes his or her services available to the relevant market;	• The extent to which the worker makes his or her services available to the relevant market;
• How the business pays the worker; and	• How the business pays the worker; and
• The extent to which the worker can realize a profit or incur a loss	• The extent to which the worker can realize a profit or incur a loss
Relationship of Parties	
Employee	**Independent Contractor**
Worker unable to perform similar work duties with other businesses, business provides worker with employee-type benefits, such as insurance, a pension plan, vacation pay, or sick pay, business has contract which describes nature of worker's functions	Worker has a narrowly defined relationship to perform a specific service and worker may perform similar services to other businesses at the same time

• **Overstating Deductions**—Figuring out your deductions is not an exact science, and most of what is allowable is subjective. But it's the IRS that gets the final word on what is allowable. So always be careful about what you are claiming; make sure it is a legitimate expense that is directly related to your business. The deductions you claim must be reasonable and responsible. In addition, you have to be ready to *prove* the deducted items are used for work. If you're caught screwing up on deductions, you'll owe the original tax amount, plus interest and penalties.

If you run into one (or more) of these problems, remember that you have options. As always, consult with a tax professional. I know I say this a lot, but when you're sick, you go to a doctor, and when your taxes are sick, you go to a tax specialist. It's as simple as that. Beyond that, you always have time—even when the IRS comes calling and puts you on notice. By law, you have sixty days from when you get a notice from the IRS to file an appeal. Appealing will buy you time, and time is your ally in a tax case.

Self-Help: Operating Your Own Business

I've got to admit it—I like being my own boss. I'd bet that most entrepreneurs would say the same thing.

But running your own show isn't all strawberries and whipped cream. As I've already shown you, there are myriad tax issues to wrestle with when you own your own business.

Fear not. From my own experience—and from hanging out with lots of other business owners—I've learned a great deal about small businesses and taxes. Let's take some time here to lay out basic tax tips for the newly self-employed:

- Set up a separate bank account and credit card for your business income and expenses. And reconcile both accounts on a regular basis (at least once per month). This will make your accounting work easier at the end of the year.
- Don't use your business bank account or credit card for personal transactions and vice versa. Yes, this seems like a pretty obvious offshoot of the first tip listed. However, I have seen this problem occur time and time again, so it is worth mentioning explicitly.

- Come tax time, use Schedule C or other business-related tax return to work out your income-minus-expenses equation. Most folks don't make much profit when they are first starting out, but if you do, it will increase your taxable income and the amount of self-employment tax you must pay. On the flip side of that coin, if you lost money or spent more than you made, it will reduce the amount of taxes you must pay.

- Keep organized records of all of your business-related income. It's best to record every dime as soon as you receive payment. Getting in the habit of using even a simple invoice and receipt system will help you track your earnings.

- Remember, the IRS gets copies of your 1099s and other income statements, so make sure you are 100 percent accurate in your reporting of all income.

- Get receipts for every business expense, even cash ones, and keep them in a place where they won't be easily destroyed.

- If you use your home or apartment for an office, you may be able to deduct a portion of your mortgage or rent. There are two basic requirements for your home to qualify as a deduction: 1) you must regularly use part of your home exclusively for business and it must be a separately identifiable space; 2) you must be able to show that your home is your principal place of business.

- Keep track of standard business deductions, such as advertising, business cards, website expenses, office supplies, computer equipment, and maintenance. If you pay dues or subscription fees related to your field, those can be deducted, along with certain types of insurance and legal fees. It may also be possible to deduct business-related interest paid on loans or equipment. If you work out of your home office, highlight business-related long distance telephone calls on your monthly telephone bills.

- Travel expenses related to your business may be deductible, along with some meals. Keep track of your mileage as well. It helps to keep a notebook in your car to record business trips.
- If you pay for your own health insurance, you can deduct the full cost of your premiums.
- If you rent office space, that counts, along with utility bills and phone expenses. Just be sure to record business calls separately from personal ones if you use your home or cell phone for both purposes.
- Don't let your well-meaning neighbor tell you that if you do work via the Internet for a client in another country that you don't have to pay taxes on it. The U.S. Tax Code states that if you live in the United States and earn money, you need to pay taxes on it. It doesn't matter if your client is in Canada or Calcutta.

Business Credits or Deductions to Which You May Be Entitled

The good news for you as a small business owner is that you do get some excellent tax breaks from the government.

Here are some of my favorites:

- **Sales and Use Tax Exemptions**—Based on the state you are located in, you may be able to claim sales tax exemptions for certain business purchases. Exemptions vary from state to state and also by the type of business. For example, some states will allow you to purchase manufacturing equipment without paying any sales tax on it. You can find more information for your state from either the Department of Revenue or the Department of Taxation.

- **Manufacturing**—You may be able to take credits or deductions at the federal and state levels for new manufacturing equipment that you purchase to run your business. In some states, namely California, Illinois, and New York, you will receive a credit toward the cost of new equipment.

- **Production Activity**—As of 2010, if more than 50 percent of your products are made in the United States, you are entitled to a federal tax deduction. The amount will equal 10 percent of the individual business owner's adjusted gross income or 10 percent of income received from those products sold. A few states—Pennsylvania, Virginia, and Vermont to name a few—also offer the same percentage of deduction from state taxes.

- **Research and Development**—If you conduct R&D, you may qualify to have 20 percent of your research expenses refunded to you on a state and federal level. This is not a permanent tax credit, but President Obama is proposing that it be made permanent. Many biotechnology companies set up shop in states like California, New Jersey, Pennsylvania, and Ohio because they offer additional tax incentives for R&D companies. In fact, in Pennsylvania and New Jersey, biotech companies are eligible to sell their credits.

Tax Implications of Selling Your Business

I don't want to sell my business—I love what I'm doing so much—but some day, who knows? That's what any good entrepreneur thinks—we don't want to sell, but we're not taking the option off the table in the future.

If and when you decide the time is right to sell your business, remember that your business resembles pieces of a puzzle more than a uniform, one-piece business. In tax lawyer terms, that means your company is not really one singular entity but rather is made up of several assets. The assets are actually sold separately in order to determine gains and losses.

In a sale, business assets will be classified as:

- Real property
- Depreciable property
- Capital assets
- Property or inventory offered for sale to customers

Any inventory sold would still be considered either ordinary income or a loss. Capital assets would result in either a capital gain or a loss. If you have real or depreciable property that you have used in the business for longer than one year, the sale of that property could result in either a loss or a gain through what the IRS calls a Section 1231 transaction.

There are many issues to consider when selling your business, and I can't stress how important the advice of a business law attorney is to ensuring the sale is completed properly. Consider the following when selling your business:

For Partnerships

If your business is a partnership, the IRS considers it a capital asset. Gains and losses from unrealized inventory items or receivables are treated as ordinary gains or losses.

For Corporations

If you have interest in a corporation, it is usually represented by the amount of stock certificates you hold. You'll realize a capital gain or, with the way business has been going lately, you may realize a capital loss when you sell your stock.

Tax Implications of Closing Your Business

Hey, it's a tough economy out there. So it's no shame if you hung out your shingle a while back but financial events outside your control have conspired to rob your fledgling company of the cash it needs to keep percolating.

But what if you decide to cut your losses and close your business without selling it or filing for bankruptcy? Then what do you do?

Well, it is possible for you to abandon your business legally. But that doesn't mean just locking the doors and walking away, something I've seen more and more here in California.

From a tax perspective, you'll need to show your ordinary losses (such as simple operating losses or inventory that you sold below cost) and your capital losses (losses resulting from the sale of an investment, such as a stock or bond). Ordinary losses are 100 percent deductible against your ordinary income, whereas capital losses are used first to offset capital gains, then up to $3,000 in losses can be deducted against ordinary income. By showing that your business's losses outweigh its profits, you are essentially showing that your business endeavor is insolvent.

Aside from showing losses, there is a legitimate way to close a business. You'll need to file a final annual return for the actual year that you go out of business. The following checklist outlines the things you must do and forms you must file to properly close out your business.

IRS Checklist for Closing a Business:

1. Make your final federal tax deposits (Form 8109-B).
2. File your final quarterly or annual employment tax form (Forms 940, 941, and 943 or 943-A if they apply).
3. Issue your final wage and withholding information to employees (Form W-2).
4. Report information from W-2s issued (Form W-3).
5. File final tip income and allocated tips information return if this applies (Form 8027).
6. Report capital gains or losses (Form 1040, 1065, or 1120).

7. Report a partner's and/or shareholder's share if this applies (Form 1065 or 1120S).
8. File final employee pension and benefit plan information (Form 5500).
9. Issue final payment information to any sub-contractors (Form 1099-MISC).
10. Report information from any 1099s issued (Form 1096).
11. Report corporate dissolution or liquidation (Form 966).
12. Consider allowing your S Corporation election to terminate if this applies (Form 1120S).
13. Report any business asset sales (Form 8594).
14. Report the sale or exchange of property used in your trade or business (Form 4797).

Filing Rules for Inactive Companies

A lot of entrepreneurs have shuttered money-losing businesses in the last few years.

So, once a business is rendered "inactive," are taxes still owed on your now "out of business" business?

The Number One Best Way to Avoid Back Taxes for Small Business Owners

There are plenty of ways to avoid paying the IRS taxes, and some ideas are better than others. One I really like is both easy and obvious. What is it? Simple: just review your taxes before filing them. Look over your taxes and make sure all your income is accounted for. It can save you from having to pay a lot of money later in the form of back taxes.

You'd be amazed how many otherwise smart people don't review their tax forms.

Sure, your company may have earned no income before you shut it down, but a lot of states have what the IRS refers to as "minimum franchise taxes." These taxes are akin to an annual fee/tax for the privilege of being able to say you are an incorporated entity in the state.

The IRS also wants you to adhere to filing requirements, even if it's just to show that you did no business. Once formed, a corporation has ongoing maintenance requirements even if you're out of state and not using it.

Contact a reputable tax specialist familiar with business issues to see if there's a way to streamline the tax filing process (in light of the lack of activity) and to avoid any penalties and interest that might have accrued.

Tax Implications of Filing Bankruptcy for Your Business

You may have done everything you could to keep your business afloat during the financial meltdown. Despite your good intentions, you may have found yourself considering bankruptcy as a way out of the mounting bills that are taking up space in your office. Well, you certainly aren't alone. Millions of business owners across the country are facing difficult decisions just like this.

First rule? File your taxes. It doesn't matter if you file Chapter 7, 11, 12, or 13 bankruptcies; you will still need to file all of your federal, state, and local tax returns, both business and personal. If you fail to do this or request an extension, your bankruptcy petition may be converted to a different chapter or dismissed entirely. And the tax rules vary depending on the type of bankruptcy protection for which you apply.

Keep in mind that just because you file for bankruptcy, it doesn't mean you get a free ride. Generally, when you owe money and the debt is forgiven or cancelled, the amount owed becomes taxable income.

However, if the debt is cancelled through a bankruptcy filing, then that money is not considered income. The downside is that it could also reduce other tax benefits to which you might be entitled. For example, you can't claim deductions for assets liquidated through the bankruptcy proceedings.

Here are some other things you'll need to know about the IRS and the U.S. Bankruptcy Code:

- For Chapter 13 specifically, you must file all tax returns within a four-year period of the bankruptcy filing date.
- If your corporation files Chapter 11, it doesn't mean that your tax debt is discharged automatically, particularly if you filed a false return or intentionally tried to evade paying taxes.
- Under a Chapter 13 discharge, the following items are not dischargeable through the bankruptcy proceedings: taxes where a return was not filed, withheld taxes, taxes that were not filed in a timely manner within a two-year period of the bankruptcy filing, and even taxes that a person tried to evade or otherwise get out of.
- You do not have to include cancelled debt in your gross income if cancellation takes place through a bankruptcy.
- If you have qualified real property business debt, that also does not need to be included in your gross income.

Overall, don't make the mistake of believing bankruptcy will get you out of every tax debt, every time.

It all depends on your specific situation and what type of taxes you owe. Most of the time, an officer of a corporation is not held personally liable for corporate income taxes, but the IRS has a very different perspective when it comes to past-due payroll taxes, and it will come after you if you owe them, even if you have filed for bankruptcy. Payroll taxes include federal unemployment taxes, Social Security and Medicare taxes (or FICA taxes), and federal withholding tax for your employees.

Likewise, shareholders are usually only liable for debts that are personally guaranteed. But there have been court cases where a business owner treated the business assets as his own personal assets. Once this corporate veil has been pierced and creditors have been harmed by the business owner's misuse of funds, then that owner, and any other owners or shareholders, can be held personally liable for the business debt.

In the long run, take it from the Tax Lady; try not to fall behind on your business taxes. If you do find yourself in that situation and you are not yet at the bankruptcy stage, consider contacting the IRS to work out a payment arrangement. If you show them you are sincerely trying to make an effort to pay you may be granted a thirty to sixty day extension. You could also try to take out a loan from your bank or sell off some personal assets to come up with the cash you need to stay out of hot water with the IRS.

Implications of Past-Due Taxes on Your Business

Most times, business owners won't be facing something as severe as bankruptcy, but they may be facing a back tax problem.

If you are a small business owner and you find that you're behind on your taxes, know what you're up against and craft a plan to pay the money back.

First, know that the IRS offers several programs to business taxpayers (all taxpayers, for that matter) who owe back taxes. They all can help your case; some are better than others. The most common programs are the Offer in Compromise, Installment Agreement, and Currently Not Collectible Status. I'll discuss those options in greater detail in chapter 9.

Before you can qualify for any of these three "get out of trouble" programs, you have to be fully compliant with your tax obligations.

For business taxpayers, compliance has three major components:

1. **File all taxes:** The IRS will require the business to file all past-due tax returns before considering a resolution.
2. **Payroll compliance:** The second requirement is that any open business with employees must be in compliance with its payroll deposit requirement. In most cases, the IRS wants you to get and remain in compliance for two consecutive quarters before it will agree to any back taxes resolution.
3. **Estimated tax payments:** The third requirement is that non-organized businesses (e.g., sole proprietorships, self-employed, etc.) are not treated as separate taxable entities from their owners. As a result, the owner must be up to date on his or her estimated tax payments on the current tax year.

Tax Tips to Keep the IRS at Bay

Here are some more tax tips for small business owners that will help keep the IRS out of your wallet:

- Stay current on business and payroll taxes.
- If money is tight, cut expenses and collect payments owed to keep cash flow alive.
- Be truthful about existing debts when applying for a new loan or consolidating existing loans.
- Open checking and savings accounts at a bank other than the bank to which your company may owe money.
- Don't borrow from the company pension plan because of steep penalties and the possibility of disqualification of the plan.
- Think about returning some leased property if you can work without it.
- If you are running into money problems, consider selling the business and use the cash to repay debtors. When things look up, you can regroup and start again.

The estimated tax payments are an estimate on the taxes due on the income made by the business through the year.

Be alert and honest with yourself. If you don't pay your taxes in a timely manner and you don't bother to let the IRS know why you are unable to pay your taxes, it is entitled to start enforcement action against you and your business. Enforcement actions can include a levy against income and other assets or a Trust Fund Recovery Penalty if you have not paid employment taxes or paid them late. Other collection action can include mandatory monthly payments of payroll taxes instead of paying them quarterly and placing the withheld amounts in a special bank account to avoid prosecution. In some cases, the IRS can even shutter your business until you get your tax debts in order.

Here's a good tip on the payroll issue. Aim to set aside at least 13 percent on top of your company's gross payroll to cover payroll taxes in order to avoid facing payroll tax problems.

What's New in Taxes Based on the Economic Stimulus Act

Recent events, the result of a political switch in Washington, have changed the small business tax landscape—and most of that has to do with the recently enacted Economic Stimulus Act.

The $780 billion financial package was geared toward getting the U.S. economy back on its feet, mostly from shovel-ready projects and funding for things like clean energy and selected public works projects. The effectiveness of the stimulus package is still up for debate. However, in the meantime, it does include some pieces that may help your business continue operating in these murky economic waters. Changes include:

- **Increased Section 179 deduction limits**—Section 179 is a part of the IRS code that allows business owners to deduct the cost of certain types of property from their income taxes as long as the property is used for business. For tax years beginning in 2008, the amount has increased to $250,000 (or $285,000 for qualified enterprise zone or renewal community property). The phase-out amount has also been increased to $800,000.

- **Special depreciation allowances for certain types of qualified property**—The Stimulus Act makes the special depreciation allowance available in every state. Items that qualify for an additional first-year special depreciation include off-the-shelf computer software, water utility property, qualified leasehold improvement property, and tangible property that depreciate under MACRS (the modified accelerated cost recovery system) with twenty years or less for the recovery period. There are restrictions about what will qualify, so it's best to review the full guidelines on the IRS website.

- **Business vehicle depreciation limits**—If you use a vehicle that is not a van or truck during the course of your business and it was first placed in service during 2010, you may be able to take a depreciation deduction of $3,060. If you have a truck or van, the depreciation deduction is $3,160. The amounts are higher if the special depreciation allowance applies to you. One caveat—these limits only apply if the vehicle is used for business 100 percent of the time; if you use the vehicle for less time than that, the amounts are reduced.

Roni's Words of Wisdom

I've found that the best remedy for avoiding back taxes is to stay ahead of the game, keep on paying (until you just can't pay anymore), and to be up-front and honest about where you stand and what needs to be done.

The IRS is a tough nut to crack, and it's my opinion that you can't do it alone. So, if you find yourself in hot water with the government, hire a good tax professional, get your records together, and take advantage of every tip I've laid out for you in this chapter.

Dealing with back taxes really requires having a "no stone unturned" mindset. Examine every potential loophole and explore every possible solution.

Chances are you can beat the IRS or at least hang in there and outlast it by sheer strength of will. Either way, increasing your knowledge and getting good tax help will keep your business in good shape, even during a recession.

7

Experiencing a Personal Crisis? News Flash: Don't Expect Any Sympathy from Uncle Sam

Benjamin Franklin said that nothing in this world is certain except death and taxes. When death is not an option and the world is maximizing the uncertainty, taxes look like an intriguing career alternative.

— JAMES BARRON,
NEW YORK TIMES REPORTER

As a business owner, a woman, and a plugged-in community advocate, I've grown accustomed to a hectic lifestyle.

In fact, it's become almost a badge of honor to be so busy that you can't keep track of everything going on in your life. I'm no different. And sometimes, *hectic* doesn't begin to cover it. When you are facing a personal crisis, you can count on friends and family to help lighten the load, but if you're hoping the IRS will make your life any easier, you need to think again.

It's something I see every day. People get into trouble with the IRS for lots of reasons—things that happen in everyday life. It's not your fault; things happen that are beyond your control. Regardless, a personal crisis like a divorce, a death in the family, or a serious illness can have a ripple effect on your life that can, among other disasters, draw the ire and focus of the Internal Revenue Service.

The Tax Impact of a Personal Crisis

In these tough times, it seems like everywhere you look someone is dealing with a personal crisis. I don't use the word *crisis* lightly. What else would you call a situation wherein you can no longer pay for life's necessities? What do you call it when the family breadwinner suddenly loses his or her job?

This scenario is so familiar these days that it's almost become a cliché. Even so, it's the stark reality for millions of families across the country. It's not just the terrifying unemployment rates, either. The increasing frequency of chronic illnesses and expensive medical treatments that are often not covered by insurance are other factors for so many families. Or devastation hits in the form of the death of a spouse.

How about the elderly couple who never did any estate planning, counting on the equity in their home to act as their nest egg? Well, that nest egg is suddenly worth a whole lot less than it was a few years back. Now they have no idea how they'll get by during their golden years.

Or how about the couple that winds up divorced or is so buried in debt that bankruptcy is the only way to keep from sinking into the financial abyss? It doesn't matter if their situation was triggered by their own mistake or by forces outside their control. The result is the same: complete devastation.

Divorce, unexpected health problems, a death in the family, personal bankruptcy, and poor estate planning are all personal crises that most of us would prefer to avoid. In this economy, however, intentions don't mean much. I'm willing to bet that you or someone you know and love is experiencing at least one of these problems.

Don't expect the IRS to give you a shoulder to cry on.

Let's take a look at some statistics for each of these personal crises, focusing directly on the most common ones: divorce, death in the family, and a medical crisis, along with a way out of each situation from a tax point of view.

Take Care of Yourself

No matter where you are with the IRS, if you are experiencing a personal crisis, there is no reason to go it alone.

Turn to your friends, family, and neighbors. Chances are, they want to help but don't know how. Not comfortable asking your loved ones for help? Community organizations are always standing by to provide material assistance, counseling, and education.

Divorce

According to Americans for Divorce Reform, approximately 40–50 percent of all marriages will end in divorce. Some estimates claim rates as high as 60 percent. And for second marriages, somewhere between 60 and 80 percent will end in divorce. With those odds, it's a wonder anyone ties the knot anymore.

There is a silver lining, though. Oddly enough, there are those who believe this lousy economy is actually helping to lower the divorce rate. Are people getting along better? Well, maybe, but most experts agree that it's the expenses associated with a divorce that are forcing more couples to stick together—expenses like attorney fees, having to buy out your spouse's portion of a home, child support, alimony, dividing assets, etc.

Now, add in the grim fact that one spouse may have recently been laid off, and suddenly divorce looks harder than shelving your differences and staying in the marriage for a while longer. After all, two people can live more cheaply than one—provided the situation isn't unbearable.

Hey, it's no fun to be forced to stay in a bad situation, and marriages that are truly broken won't heal by sticking it out through tough financial times. On the other hand, sometimes pushing through the tough times might actually strengthen your relationship, and you can emerge stronger, having survived a financial crisis together.

Tax Implications of Divorce

If you're struggling through a divorce, my heart goes out to you and to your family. Going through a divorce is tough on everyone involved. And all the disappointment and hurt can turn any couple bitter. But it's important to put aside your differences and get your tax situation straightened out. Here's a guide on the most basic things to work out.

Income Tax

The IRS is pretty clear that there are just two ways that a couple who are legally married at the end of the tax year can file their taxes. You can either file *jointly* or you can file a *married filing separate* return.

If you file your taxes together, remember that you both are responsible for anything either of you got wrong on your taxes. This is based on the concept of *joint and several liability*. That simply means that two or more individuals are each individually responsible for the full payment of the same tax debt. In the case of a federal tax debt, a joint and several liability usually arises when a married couple files a joint tax return. If your husband was evading taxes during the marriage, you can be held liable for the tax debt, including interest and penalties. The IRS will, as usual, get its money. It can collect the entire amount of the joint tax debt from one or both spouses. For example, if Mr. and Mrs. Taxpayer owe $5,000 jointly to the IRS, the

IRS can collect the full $5,000 from either Mr. Taxpayer or Mrs. Taxpayer, or part of the $5,000 from both Mr. and Mrs. Taxpayer. Even if a divorce decree states one of them is solely responsible for the tax debt, the IRS can still hold both spouses accountable. The good news—if you can call it that—is that the IRS cannot collect more than is actually owed.

Why is joint and several liability such an important concept? Because it allows the IRS to collect a joint tax debt from more than one source. So, if you enter into an arrangement with the IRS to relieve all or part of a joint liability, the IRS can (and usually will) go after your ex for the remaining balance. The IRS will use all available means, including wage garnishments, bank levies, federal tax liens, and asset seizures, to collect a tax debt. If a taxpayer and a former spouse jointly owe the IRS, it is important that each have a formal arrangement with the IRS, whether it is achieved by filing an Offer in Compromise, establishing an Installment Agreement, or requesting Currently Not Collectible status.

Now what if your spouse was engaged in some shady tax dealings, and you legitimately had no idea? There is some relief available through *Innocent Spouse Relief.* It's no piece of cake, but if you can prove that you were an innocent party to your spouse's financial and tax shenanigans, the IRS may release you from liability. But remember the burden of proving you were not involved or aware of the improper claims is entirely on you. That's why I often tell clients who mistrust their spouses that it may be best to file separate returns to protect themselves in the long run, especially if there are children from a prior marriage or a previous tax debt.

Innocent, Your Honor

It happens all the time. A divorced man or woman gets an unexpected surprise from his or her previous marriage: an IRS tax liability. Fortunately, federal tax law provides these unfortunate folks with possible relief under the Innocent Spouse program.

It takes work, and you have to put in the time, but by requesting Innocent Spouse consideration, you can be relieved of responsibility for paying taxes, interest, and penalties if your spouse improperly reported items or omitted items on your joint tax return. You have only two years after the date of the first collection attempt to file for Innocent Spouse Relief.

According to the IRS, the following conditions must be met before Innocent Spouse Relief will be granted:

- You filed a joint return that has incorrect information relating to your spouse.
- You prove that, at the time you signed the joint return, you did not know, and had no reason to know, that there was an error on the return.
- The IRS determines that, given all of the facts, it would be unfair to hold you responsible for the errors on the return.

Note that ignorance really is bliss in this case. The IRS states that if you knew about the error at the time the return was prepared and filed, you do not qualify for Innocent Spouse Relief.

A Step-by-Step Guide to Innocent Spouse Relief

Divorce is difficult enough to deal with; now you have to cope with a tax debt? Worse yet, you didn't do anything wrong, your ex did. Talk about adding insult to injury!

If you find yourself in that situation, and I've seen it happen many times, Innocent Spouse Relief can save you a world of trouble. Here's a step-by-step guide to claiming Innocent Spouse Relief:

- **Step One: Find Out if You're Eligible**—Your first order of business is to determine whether you meet the conditions for qualification:

1. You filed a joint return showing an understatement of tax, resulting from incorrect items (such as understated income or overstated deductions).
2. You can show that at the time you signed the joint return, you were not aware that the information was incorrect, and that you had no reason to know.
3. After reviewing all the facts, it would be unfair to hold you liable for the tax debt.
4. You have not been part of any fraudulent tax activities.

- **Step Two: File the Form**—To claim Innocent Spouse Relief, you will need to fill out Form 8857. The form asks for information about the tax years from which you are requesting relief, some basic information about you and your spouse (or ex-spouse), the nature of your relationship now, how finances were handled in that relationship, and your state of mind at the time the taxes were filed. Although this information is awfully personal, it is required to determine if you knew, or should have known, that the taxes were incorrect.

- **Step Three: State Your Case**—In addition to filing Form 8857, you will need to provide any documentation and evidence you might have. Every little bit helps, so make sure you hang on to those pay stubs, receipts, and any correspondence that shows you weren't aware of your spouse's tax shenanigans. Just be sure to send copies of everything; the IRS is notorious for losing documents, so sending in the originals can be risky.

- **Step Four: Wait for an Answer**—The IRS sure can take its time when that suits it. You may be waiting up to six months to get a response to your request.

  - If your request is accepted, congratulations!
  - If 120 days pass without hearing anything, you have a couple of options: you can resubmit your form and

back-up documentation or you can hire a tax professional to make your case.

- If your request is denied, don't worry; many are. You can
  hire a tax professional and remake your case.

Home Ownership

Your home is probably the most expensive asset to deal with when
going through a divorce. First, you should know that generally, you
can transfer ownership of your primary residence from one spouse
to the other because of the divorce and the IRS will not consider that
a taxable event.

So, how do you divvy it all up fairly? It all depends on your specific
situation and divorce settlement. The most common methods are:

- You can sell the home and divide the profit as you see fit.
- You can buy out your spouse's share of the home, or vice
  versa.
- If the housing market is shaky (much like our housing market for the last few years!), you can hold on to the property for now and then sell it when the market rebounds and
  divide the profits equitably.

Selling a personal residence involves some very specific tax rules.
If your home was your primary residence for at least two of the last
five years, and you reinvest the proceeds into another home, you
should not be subject to capital gains taxes when you sell it. The IRS
gives you two years to purchase another home from the proceeds
of the sale on the former one before it will come looking for capital
gains taxes. Again, this only applies to a primary residence.

There could be an unpleasant surprise if one spouse continues to
live in the house two years or more after divorcing. The other spouse
may be liable for significant capital gains taxes when the house is
eventually sold, because the primary or principal residence rule no

longer applies. Additionally, property transfer taxes are usually paid by the spouse who is selling the house.

Spousal Support

Alimony or spousal support is generally viewed as a deduction for the person who pays it and income for the person receiving it, though this can vary based on your divorce settlement. If you are awarded spousal support, make sure you pay quarterly estimated taxes on the income, because taxes are not withheld from the payments. Doing so will ensure you don't have a nasty tax bill come April 15th.

Child Support

The IRS does not consider child support payments to be taxable income for the recipient, nor are the payments deductible by the person making the payments. As to who gets to claim the dependent exemptions for the kids, the rules vary by state. For example, in Pennsylvania, a judge can decide to award the tax break to either spouse, depending upon their respective incomes and how the tax consequences weigh out. If no specific order is made as part of the custody or divorce settlement, the default solution is to award the dependency exemption to the person who has physical custody of the children. If you have equally shared custody, you should speak with either your divorce attorney or a tax attorney to see how you should proceed.

Investment Assets

This category can get tricky. Any financial instruments that you acquire during the course of your marriage will need to be divided when you are divorcing. If the solution is to liquidate the asset, any profits will be subject to capital gains taxes. You'll want to talk to your divorce attorney and a qualified financial advisor before deciding how to divvy up these assets. Investments are handled much the same way as the sale of a home; if you want to sell the assets, whether they are stocks, bonds, or mutual funds, then your spouse will need to buy out your share. The potentially frustrating part is that the spouse being bought out gets his or her money tax-free.

And don't forget about other investment assets like expensive artwork, boats, jewelry, gold, and any other items that might depreciate in value and will need to be divided in the process of the divorce.

Retirement Accounts

I know it doesn't seem fair that your IRA or 401(k) should be parsed out, but your soon-to-be-ex spouse may be eligible to receive a part of your retirement nest egg. The IRS has some pretty strict rules that determine how the money is divided. Generally, for 401(k)s, your spouse should still get the same amount he or she would have gotten if you remained married.

IRAs, on the other hand, are a little different. If money was contributed during the course of the marriage, then each spouse will be entitled to a portion of the assets. The assets can be transferred tax-free through the divorce decree, but all the funds must be rolled over into another IRA right away to avoid paying the 20 percent federal income tax withholding penalty.

Debt

Divorce is never a happy event, but figuring out who will repay which debt can make it even nastier. If your spouse has a nasty credit card habit, you probably wonder why you should have to pay back the debts. The thing is, once you get married you are also married to each other's debts. So even if you had nothing to do with the spending, you're still on the hook for repayment.

Your best course of action is to pull your own credit report along with your spouse's and make a list of all outstanding debts. If you are on civil terms with your soon-to-be ex, you can probably work together to create a fair and logical arrangement. If things are less than pleasant between you and your spouse, then you should probably work through a mediator or your respective attorneys. No matter why the marriage is ending, you should take responsibility for your own debts and try to pay as much off as possible before the divorce is finalized. That way you can both start over with a clean slate.

How You Can File as "Head of Household"

No question, divorce is an expensive proposition—for both parties.

One way to keep a little more money in your pocket is to file your taxes as Head of Household. This tax status can save you as much as $8,000 per year on your taxes. Of course, there are rules for qualifying as Head of Household:

- You must be unmarried at the end of the year or live apart from your spouse for more than six months;
- You must maintain a household for your child (even if you do not claim him or her as a dependent), or a dependent parent, or other qualifying dependent relative;
- The household must be your home and generally must also be the main home of the qualifying dependent (i.e., they live there more than half the year);
- You must provide more than half the cost of maintaining the household; and
- You must be a U.S. citizen or resident alien for the entire tax year.

Medical/Health Problems

According to the Insurance Information Institute, 43 percent of all people aged forty and over will suffer from a long-term injury or illness that will likely last ninety days or more by the time they are sixty-five. That's almost half of all middle-aged people in this country!

Health problems can hit anyone at any time, and the effects can be catastrophic. It puts a strain on everyone in the family, and between loss of income and a pile of medical bills, it certainly puts a strain on your finances.

I'm no health nag, but based on that statistic, I'd say now is a good time to remind you to watch your weight, exercise, eat healthy, and quit smoking. Your health is one of your most valuable assets, and even minor health problems can increase your medical insurance rates or keep you from getting private coverage if you don't have access to a company-sponsored plan at work.

But even the best health insurance will not save you from the perils of lost income. If you work for a large company, they may offer you disability insurance along with your regular health insurance; policies are generally inexpensive and this type of coverage offers peace of mind. If you become disabled, health insurance should cover some of your medical bills while disability insurance can help you pay your other living expenses if you're unable to work.

Those of you hoping that Social Security Insurance or government disability will take care of you, here's a little dose of reality for you. Social Security Insurance usually only kicks in if your condition is expected to last at least twelve months and will preclude you from working at all. And with our government warning that Social Security funds will be completely gone before you know it, I certainly wouldn't bet my life on them.

Tax Implications of Health Problems

Let's be honest, if you or your family is dealing with a significant health issue, there aren't many positive benefits to the situation. At the very least, you may be able to offset some of the medical bills using your taxes.

Depending upon your financial situation, you may be able to deduct your unreimbursed medical expenses. The IRS allows you to deduct any medical expenses (from prescription and over-the-counter medications to contact lenses, lab fees, and more) that exceed 7.5 percent of your annual adjusted gross income. Normally, if you have employer-provided health care, your expenses will not be high enough to get the deduction. However, the medical bills that come along with major health problems may bump your expenses high enough to take advantage of this tax break.

If you are injured on the job, workers' compensation should cover at least a portion of your lost wages. Generally, workers' comp is not considered taxable income. If your injury was the result of an auto accident, your car insurance policy may offer replacement income coverage. Make sure you review your policy and speak with your insurance agent to see if this is available. Any payments you receive from your auto insurance policy should not be taxable.

I highly recommend purchasing disability insurance. When you pay for the policy with after-tax money (meaning that the premiums are not tax deductible), the income you receive from the coverage will not be taxable. Again, disability insurance will not make up all your income, but the tax-free status can at least help you keep more cash in your pocket. On the other hand, if your employer pays your disability insurance premiums, then the IRS views it as "deferred compensation" and it is taxable at your standard tax rates.

Of course, for longer-term disability, I've already mentioned Social Security Insurance. Now, there are some very convoluted rules for taxing Social Security benefits. Yes, depending upon your total income, you may actually have to pay taxes on a portion of your benefits. If your income is between $25,000 and $35,000, then 50 percent of your benefits will be taxable. If your income is higher than $35,000, then up to 85 percent of your benefits are taxable. I highly recommend speaking with a tax professional to determine your tax liabilities for your situation.

Now, some health problems do allow you to continue working, perhaps on a modified schedule or part-time from home. You may still be able to collect disability payments for the reduction of income. The important thing to note here is that you must report all your wages and any taxable benefits you receive. Trying to keep any income "under the table" is a bad idea, can land you in some serious trouble with the IRS, and could expose you to tax penalties for the unreported income and possible insurance fraud charges. It's just not worth it.

If you become disabled at the same time you are collecting unemployment payments, you likely will not be eligible to collect federal or state disability. Once your unemployment runs out, however, you should be able to switch status with a little paperwork. Consequently, if you are unemployed because of an injury or illness, you'll need to apply for disability benefits rather than unemployment benefits. Get some professional help on this one. Try talking to an experienced insurance representative, because the amount of benefits you receive from one public or private program may impact what money you are entitled to from other programs.

State Rules on Social Security

There are two types of government disability coverage: federal disability coverage and state programs. Each state makes its own rules for state disability programs. Right now, only five states—New York, New Jersey, Rhode Island, California, and Hawaii—plus the Commonwealth of Puerto Rico offer disability programs.

In California, if you are self-employed, you can elect to pay for state disability insurance (SDI) coverage and the premium amount will be based on your profits from the previous year.

Personal Bankruptcy

In chapter 6, I had a lot to say about bankruptcy as it applies to business owners. Personal bankruptcy, on the other hand, seems to be an especially difficult pill to swallow. It's one thing to have a business go under in this dismal economy. It's another thing to watch your personal finances sink under overwhelming debt. Bankruptcy filing is unpleasant, to say the least, but it can provide a way out.

Remember, bankruptcy is not a get-out-of-jail-free card. Filing does not allow you to skip out on your debts, keep everything you have, and start over without a care in the world. Bankruptcy laws vary from state to state. For example, in Florida, you can file for bankruptcy and still keep your primary home, though you won't be able to keep income-producing properties. In other states, filing for bankruptcy may mean a lien is attached to your home and any other assets that can be used to satisfy or pay down a bankruptcy judgment.

You should also keep in mind that laws are changing and not always in the bankrupt's favor. In the past few years, bankruptcy laws have made it harder for people to simply skip out on their debts because they are short on cash. You might think that these tougher rules would have reduced the number of filings. Think again—according to the Administrative Office of the Courts, Chapter 7 bankruptcy filings have increased 73 percent since 2009. Of the 158,141 bankruptcy filings in March of 2010, 118,505, or 75 percent, were Chapter 7s and 38,241 were Chapter 13s.

Tax Implications of Bankruptcy

To say there are tax implications for declaring personal bankruptcies is an understatement akin to saying California has a bit of a cash flow problem.

But the central question I want to answer is this—can taxpayers get rid of their back tax liability through bankruptcy? And the answer to that question is a little complicated.

Both Chapter 7 and Chapter 13 bankruptcy filings may or may not discharge a federal tax debt. It all depends on how the debt was incurred and how old the debt is. Here are the basic rules for discharging tax debts through bankruptcy:

- The due date for filing a tax return is at least three years ago. Under this rule, your tax debt has to be related to a tax return that was due at least three years before you file for bankruptcy.
- The tax return was filed at least two years ago. Under the two-year rule, your tax debt must be related to a tax return filed at least two years before you file for bankruptcy.
- The tax assessment is at least 240 days old. Under the 240-day rule, the IRS has to assess any tax at least 240 days before you declare bankruptcy.
- The tax return was not fraudulent.
- The taxpayer is not guilty of tax evasion. Here, you cannot be found guilty of any intentional action in avoiding tax laws.

If your IRS debt falls within these five statutes, then your tax debt is most likely dischargeable in Chapter 7 and Chapter 13 bankruptcy petitions. Note that any tax debts incurred on unfiled tax returns are not dischargeable. According to the IRS, you may be able to discharge such debts if you retroactively file tax returns for the appropriate year.

Before you ever start the bankruptcy filing process, you really need to consult with a bankruptcy attorney. I cannot stress this enough. Bankruptcy filing is not as clear-cut and simple as you might hope, and the experience of a seasoned bankruptcy attorney will save you enormous hassle, money, and stress.

Tax Liens

If you have an existing tax lien against your property and are successful in discharging your tax debt through bankruptcy, the lien will stay in place. You see, the bankruptcy discharge simply removes your personal obligation to pay the debt, not the IRS's ability to collect or seize property you owned at the time of the filing. So, if you have equity in any "exempt property," such as your home, your vehicles, or a pension, it may not have to be surrendered to creditors for the bankruptcy. However, the IRS may still be able to collect against these assets. Doesn't seem quite right, does it?

Gauge the Impact

When you're weighing the pros and cons of declaring bankruptcy, you need to do what's right for you, your family, and your finances. Just be sure to make an informed decision.

Although filing for bankruptcy can help you get back on your financial feet, it also has some lasting consequences. Certainly, declaring bankruptcy has become more common in recent years. However, there is still a negative connotation associated with it. And it's not just the judgment of others, as many people report feelings of personal shame. So, there are significant emotional consequences.

Aside from the emotional components, the biggest consequence of a bankruptcy filing is the impact on your credit. A bankruptcy filing will stay on your credit report for at least seven years. This can make it difficult to get a loan or secure funding for a house, a car, even a new business venture. What credit you can get will likely be at significantly higher interest rates, making it much more expensive.

However, the difficulty of getting credit may be a good thing. If you've got the shackles on credit-wise, you won't be able to rely on loans and credit cards to make ends meet. Instead, you'll have to focus on saving up for purchases and living within your means.

Again, if bankruptcy is the answer for your specific financial situation, then go for it. Just make sure you've taken the consequences into consideration.

Options Beyond Bankruptcy

If tax debt is your only source of financial turmoil, then I would caution you to look for alternatives to bankruptcy. Bankruptcy's lasting impact is an awfully high price to pay when IRS tax debt is your only problem. Instead, consult with a competent tax professional. Some even offer a free and confidential tax debt analysis in which your situation will be analyzed and a determination made as to the form of tax debt resolution for which you qualify. If your situation makes you eligible for an Offer in Compromise, I highly recommend you take it. Unlike bankruptcy, an Offer in Compromise will discharge a federal tax lien and is not reported on an individual's credit report. Furthermore, an OIC can discharge tax debts regardless of the age of the tax debts.

Burgeoning Bankruptcy

To get a clear picture of how bankruptcies are growing in the United States, let's look at the hard numbers.

U.S. personal bankruptcies reached 1.45 million by the end of 2009, compared with nearly 1.1 million filings in 2008. The estimated number of filings we will see in 2010 is 1.75 million.

To be fair, most folks who file bankruptcy have a valid reason for their financial woes. According to Elizabeth Warren, educator at Harvard Law School and author of *The Fragile Middle Class: Americans in Debt*, more than 91 percent of all people who file for bankruptcy have been affected by a serious financial crisis like divorce, job loss, or a major health problem. In fact, two-thirds have lost their jobs and at least half had serious medical problems and the bills that followed.

Death

As I've said before, there are two things you can never avoid entirely—death and taxes. And if your loved one dies and leaves you with a hefty tax bill, don't expect the IRS to send you a sympathy card.

According to a *Legal Mojo* article, more than 70 percent of Americans will die without a will. Only about 32 percent of African Americans and 26 percent of Hispanics have wills. Depending on what state you live in and how much your estate is worth, your loved ones could end up sharing everything evenly, whether you want it that way or not, on top of paying federal estate taxes. Having a will in place can help avoid complications.

Tax Implications of Death

The good news is that, generally speaking, money you inherit is not subject to federal income tax. Once the money has been transferred to your name, you are responsible for paying taxes on any investment interest it earns.

If you, your spouse, relative, or loved one dies without a will, the estate, no matter how small, will be handled through a process called intestacy law. The rules vary by state, but it's possible that a surviving spouse will have to share the assets of the estate with the children, whether he or she wants to or not. For this reason, it's vital that you draw up at least a basic will. It also helps to name a beneficiary and/or executor to carry out your final wishes. Otherwise, the probate court will appoint someone to settle your estate.

Another aspect to keep in mind is the deceased's final tax return. Just because people have passed on, it does not mean their tax obligations have passed. The IRS requires a final tax return to be filed, usually by the executor of the estate. Without an executor, the deceased's spouse or other surviving family members will be held responsible for closing out all dealings with the IRS.

The tax forms required are the same ones the deceased person was responsible for in life. However, the word *deceased* should be written next to the person's name. The taxable income of the deceased person can be reported and taxed on either his or her final return or on the return of the person who will receive the income from the estate. If there are a lot of assets or if the deceased person's taxes were fairly complicated, you are probably better off hiring a tax or estate attorney to help with all the required paperwork.

If the person had any sort of investment income, it's important to know that only income that is received up until the date and time of death should be included on the tax return. But if your spouse or relative left the investments to you, any earnings that occur after the death are your responsibility to claim on your tax return. For this reason, it is important to change formal ownership of any accounts that have been willed to you as quickly as possible after the death.

The Death Tax

One of the most onerous ideas ever to come out of Washington—a place that's a veritable breeding ground for bad ideas—is the estate tax (otherwise known as *the death tax*). People call it the death tax because the government comes after your money after you pass away—money on which you've already paid taxes.

For years, politicians have been trying to get the estate tax on the chopping block. Back in 2001, as part of the tax-cut legislation passed by Congress, the estate tax was supposed to be gradually phased out, culminating in complete elimination by 2010, only to reappear at the higher pre-2001 rates in 2011. Sound a bit confusing? Oh, it is, not least because everyone expected Congress to pass a law keeping estate taxes at the 2009 rates; estates exceeding $3.5 million for singles and $7 million for married couples are taxed at a maximum of 45 percent. But 2009 came to a close, and the estate tax was in fact repealed as scheduled when we rang in 2010.

At the time of this writing, America does not have an estate tax, as President Obama has allowed it to expire. If Congress does nothing during 2010, then the estate tax will come roaring back in 2011 at even higher rates—55 percent tax on estates valued at more than $1 million.

Frankly, the unknown status of the estate tax has created mass confusion in the estate planning world. Generally, estate plans are good tools to minimize the damage done by the death tax. Estate plans allow folks to plan the distribution of their assets to their family and favorite causes, among other recipients, after their death. This is usually done with financial instruments like life insurance, stock portfolios, and trusts. Smart use of these tools can reduce or even eliminate the impact of estate taxes. Estate plans are sophisticated and should be handled by reliable financial professionals, like a financial advisor or an estate-planning lawyer.

But there are some moves you can make on your own, moves that will reduce the tax bite from your estate:

- **Give your money away**—That's right, handing your money over to favorite charities or even to family members and friends while you're alive can reduce the value of your taxable estate while still ensuring the money goes to the people and causes closest to your heart. For example, individuals can give money to any number of individuals, up to $13,000 each year, without any tax consequences. Amounts greater than $13,000 are subject to the gift tax. Also, you can give money away—with no limit—tax-free when you pay someone's higher education or medical expenses directly.

- **Use your life insurance**—Life insurance can be a lifesaver for estate planning needs, especially if you plan to leave your business or some property to an heir. Your best bet?

Make sure your policy will cover the taxes on your estate; your heirs won't be faced with having to sell assets to pay the taxes. In the end, your policy will cut a tax-free check to your heirs.

Inheritance . . . Know the Tax Rules

If you've received an inheritance, good for you—and for the smart, prepared person who left you the money.

But you also have some tax issues to deal with.

For instance, although generally not considered taxable income, inheritances that are stashed away in IRAs or company retirement plans, including 401(k)s, 403(b)s, and annuities, are viewed as income to the recipient, and therefore considered taxable income. Here's what you need to know: non-spouse beneficiaries who inherit a 401(k) can roll over the money into an IRA, thus allowing heirs to diversify their distributions and tax bills over the rest of their lives.

Roni's Soapbox

No doubt about it, life has a way of throwing some inside, chin-high fastballs that you'd prefer to avoid. Unfortunately, avoiding the tough situations usually isn't an option. If you're suffering the financial consequences of a divorce, a severe health issue, a bankruptcy, or any other personal calamity, you have to pick yourself up, dust yourself off, and get back in the game. There's no other alternative.

Suffering through a personal crisis is hard enough without having the heavy hand of the IRS come down on you. Fortunately, the tax code has a few loopholes that you can leverage to keep the IRS at bay—giving you time to deal with your situation while keeping more cash in your pocket.

The simple truth is that life can turn on a dime, for better or worse. When it's for the worse, keep a cool head, follow the tips laid out in this chapter, and know that better days are ahead. I hope I offered some realistic solutions on how to survive the tax implications of one of these crises and still see a light at the end of the tunnel.

8

Using Investment Losses to Your Advantage

An investment in knowledge always pays the best interest.
—BENJAMIN FRANKLIN,
AUTHOR, PRINTER, INVENTOR, DIPLOMAT, SCIENTIST

Let's face it. It hasn't been a great run for investors lately. The stock market has lost trillions of dollars and investors' portfolios have been decimated.

The real-life ripple effect of all that money lost in the stock market is almost surreal. It's not just the big investors that are hurting. As stocks plummet, so do retirement accounts. All across the country, people are forced to delay retirement or, even worse, come out of retirement when their nest eggs run out. All that money they spent decades saving is gone in a matter of weeks.

All those delayed retirements are also impacting younger folks. The new up-and-coming workers are being boxed out of advancement opportunities by the boomers who can't afford to retire. Without those job vacancies, the younger talent find fewer job opportunities.

Unfortunately, companies are solving this problem by getting rid of older, more expensive employees and bringing in the young go-getters at lower salaries and with fewer benefits. This is just one example of the wide-reaching impact Wall Street losses have on our economy.

I know a lot of people are angry at the investment world. I understand that anger, I really do. Just remember, most of the people working in those financial companies are not the fat cat traders and executives. Wall Street companies are laying off up to 40 percent of their staff, from top executives down to receptionists. I daresay they are in the same boat we are.

Wall Street's Burden

When I need to unwind, I head to Vegas. It's one of my favorite cities, and I like the contrast between the Strip and Wall Street. Both of them will take your money, but at least Vegas is honest about it from behind all the neon lights and gaudy glamor. Wall Street, on the other hand, will throw you under the bus while collecting bailout cash from the government.

Once you embrace the cold, hard fact that the people pulling the levers on Wall Street were just as much frauds as the Wizard of Oz, then hopefully you can learn from the experience of losing money in the markets. With that hard-won knowledge fresh in your mind, you can start to recoup some of your losses through smart tax moves.

Wall Street: Tough Ride for the Bulls

On October 9, 2007, the Dow Jones Industrial Average reached a high water mark of 14,164—one that it hasn't come close to revisiting in the years since.

The months that followed, the ones leading into the Great Recession, were among the worst ever recorded in Wall Street history.

Let's look at the chronology, or as some wise guys might put it, Wall Street's version of the Bataan Death March of World War II. You can actually track the decline of the stock market in three stages:

1. October 2007 through March 2008—just after investment banking giant Bear Stearns collapsed.

    *   October 9, 2007—The Dow Jones closes at a high of 14,164.54.

2. March 2008 through December 2008—After a fall of 2,000 points, by March 2008, the Dow Jones went into a six-month tailspin. During that time, Lehman Brothers and insurance behemoth AIG failed.

    *   November 19, 2008—The Dow Jones fell below 8,000.

3. December 2008 through February 2009—During this period, the Dow lost another thousand points, as America inaugurated a new president, and Congress passed the $787 billion stimulus bill.

    *   February 23, 2009—The Dow Jones posts its lowest close since spring 1997, at 7,114.94.

In that eighteen-month period, the Dow lost $11.2 trillion. It also included six of the ten worst days in Wall Street history.

Reality Check

Of course, tax-paying Americans were paying close attention to the stock market during this period—and taking stock.

*   In 2005, prior to the tough economic times, the U.S. personal savings rate was at 0.5 percent. By May 2009, the

savings rate—to the credit of the average American—rose to 6.9 percent.

- In September 2008, total credit card debt held by Americans was at $975 billion. A year later, that number was down to $899 billion.

Clearly, Americans were shaken by the economic maelstrom.

Look, I've got a portfolio, too, and sure, I've taken my lumps. However, there is no prize for playing the blame game. So, it is really time to catch your own bearings and focus on the task at hand— restoring the lost wealth through smarter and more secure investment strategies.

One of the most apt investment strategies, given what's happened, is using your investment losses to your tax advantage. Here is how.

Your Investments and How They're Taxed

The starting point for making the most of your investment through taxes is understanding how your investments will be treated by the IRS. Depending upon your investments, you may be looking at three different tax situations.

- **Dividends**—Dividends aren't exactly free money, but they're the next best thing. Dividends are income distributions from a company's profits to its shareholders. Investors have the option of receiving the dividend in the form of a check or they can have the proceeds automatically reinvested in a dividend reinvestment plan (DRIP). Dividends are taxed at the Long Term Capital Gains Rate (0–15 percent).
- **Interest**—Interest is the amount of money you earn on a bond investment or loan. Most people don't bother to take a good look at how interest is treated by the IRS. Interest earned from your investments, mostly Treasury bonds or money

market investments, is considered taxable at your ordinary income tax rate.

- **Capital Gains and Losses**—Capital gains are a bit more confusing. Each time you sell an investment security such as a stock or bond for a profit, you generate a capital gain. If you held that investment for at least twelve months, it is called a long-term capital gain, and it's taxed at either 0 or 15 percent, depending upon your income tax bracket. If you held the investment for less than twelve months, then it's considered a short-term capital gain and is taxed at your ordinary income tax rate.

Now, if you sell an investment and lose money on the sale, a capital loss is generated. Sometimes this is a good thing. How could losing money on the sale of an investment be good for your wallet? Capital losses can be written off dollar for dollar against any capital gain. So, rather than hanging on to a "loser" stock, you can sell it and use the loss to reduce the capital gains tax you would pay on selling your "winners."

Note—losses on 401(k)s, IRAs, 529s, or other investments that you don't sell do not create capital losses.

Deducting Investment Interest

The law allows you to deduct interest on loans used to make investments, depending upon the amount of your investment income.

When totaling up your investment income to see where your limit lies, you typically can't count capital gains that get special treatment under the law. There's a reason for that and it involves our best and brightest up there in Washington. You see, Congress doesn't want to let you deduct investment interest in a higher bracket if your gains are being taxed at only 15 percent. You have the option of including your capital gains in investment income, but then you can't take advantage of the lower capital gains rates.

Tax Harvesting

As I just discussed, different forms of investment income are taxed differently. The trick is to use each tax method to your advantage. The strategy that gives you the biggest bang for your buck is harvesting your stock gains and losses to give you the maximum income with a minimum of taxes. This revolves around the capital gains and losses rules.

How Tax Harvesting Works

Tax harvesting is probably best explained as a step-by-step process. Essentially, it all boils down to three key moves:

- Balance net capital gains and losses.
- Offset losses against ordinary income.
- Know your wash sales rules.

Balancing Net Gains and Losses

Toward the end of every year, take a look at your stock portfolio. Tally up all sales that resulted in a capital gain, then tally up your losses. If you have more gains than losses (not easy to do in this economy!), you are facing up to 15 percent in capital gains taxes. Rather than shelling out the cash, review your remaining holdings and see if there are any losers you want to get rid of. You can deduct any losses directly from your gains and end up paying nothing in capital gains taxes at all.

It sounds a little more complicated than it is. Let's say you have a long-term capital gain of $1,000 from a sale earlier in the year. You peruse your portfolio and find a stock with a long-term capital loss of $1,000. If you sell that stock, you net the $1,000 loss against the $1,000 gain; this would leave you with no capital gains taxes to worry about at all.

Taxes and Stocks

Taxes should never be the only reason you sell off an investment. You invested in the first place to make your money work for you, so if you have a stock that is taking off, by all means, keep it! Remember, you don't pay taxes on a capital investment until you sell it, so let your money continue growing.

Offset Losses Against Income

If you have capital losses for the year that exceed your capital gains—and you aren't looking to unload any winning investments—you will be thrilled to find that you can use your losses to offset ordinary income. You can deduct up to $3,000 in capital losses each year from your wages, bonuses, and any other taxable income.

For example, let's say you sold off shares of your stock mutual fund earlier in the year and lost $3,000 on the deal. If you weren't lucky enough to have any capital gains during the year (and in this economy, that scenario is frighteningly common), then you would deduct $3,000 from your income. If you are in the 25 percent tax bracket, this amounts to $750 in savings.

If your total capital loss exceeds $3,000 or exceeds your claimed ordinary income, you can carry over the unused part to the next year and treat it as if you had incurred it in that next year. This carryover can be used indefinitely until the remaining capital loss is completely used up.

Understanding the Wash Sale Rule

Before you go dumping stocks to take advantage of the capital gains and losses, you need to understand the wash sale rule. Essentially, the IRS will not allow you to claim a capital loss if you buy the same security within thirty days of the sale. This prevents investors from dumping a stock, taking a tax break, and re-buying the same stock next week. Of course, you can always repurchase the stock; just wait more than thirty days and you can have your stock and your tax deduction, too.

These simple steps are the essence of tax harvesting. Review your portfolio, compare your capital gains to your losses, and either balance them out so you are left with no capital gains taxes or use excess losses to reduce your taxable income. Of course, if you have a particularly tricky tax or investment situation, you are always better off consulting a tax professional. It may take some time and a little money, but it can end up saving you thousands of dollars in taxes.

Deduct Your Investment Expenses

Many costs associated with your investments are tax deductible. Here's a list of what you can deduct:

- The cost of investment magazines, newsletters, and books;
- The cost of trips to your financial advisor or stockbroker's office;
- Travel costs to investigate investment properties;
- Investment fees, custodial fees, trust administration fees, and other expenses you paid to maintain your taxable investments;
- Fees for online trading (restricted to account maintenance-related fees);
- Legal and accounting fees related to your investments;
- Bank and safe deposit boxes used to store investment documents; and
- Computer and software costs related to investing.

However, there are a variety of expenses you can't deduct:

- Broker's commissions;
- Wall Street-type money-making seminars;
- Costs to attend a stockholder's meeting; and
- Expenses associated with creating tax-free investment income.

Investment expenses are listed as miscellaneous expenses on Schedule A of your Form 1040. This does mean they are subject to the 2 percent adjusted gross income floor, but when added with your other miscellaneous expenses, I bet most people can take advantage of the tax break.

Take Advantage of Holding Periods

As I already mentioned, the IRS has different rules for your investments based on how long you have owned them. The clock on any investment begins the day you purchase it.

Investments you own for twelve months or longer are considered long-term investments. When you sell the investment after the twelve-month period, you get either a long-term capital gain or long-term capital loss. Investments you own for less than twelve months are considered short-term investments, creating short-term capital gains or short-term losses.

Short-term losses can be used to offset short-term gains, and long-term losses can be used to offset long-term gains. This is important to remember while evaluating your portfolio every year; you cannot use short-term losses to offset long-term gains. So make sure you are paying attention to the holding periods of each investment before you start harvesting your investments. It would be a shame to sell off an investment that will not help your tax situation at all.

Let's say you bought 100 shares of Apple on May 1, 2009. If you sold the stock on April 30, 2010, this is considered a short-term taxable event. Any profits you made on the sale would be taxed at your ordinary income tax rate.

Now, let's say instead, you sold those same shares a few days later, on May 2, 2010; this is now a long-term taxable event and is taxed at much lower rates, from 0 to 15 percent.

Collectible Losses

Stocks and bonds aren't the only investment options out there. Many people make decent income from collecting and selling stamps, rare baseball cards, and coins. These collectors spend money buying new pieces, hoping to sell them for a higher price.

Of course, just like any investment, the value of a collectible can go down as well. Remember Beanie Babies? If you spent $3,500 for "Freckles" during the height of that stuffed animal craze, today you would be lucky to unload that little leopard for a dollar at the flea market. So, is there any way to recover your lost investment?

The IRS does recognize collectibles as capital investments, so long as the items were clearly purchased for investment purposes. This may allow you either to use the loss to offset any capital gains for the year or deduct up to $3,000 worth of losses from your ordinary income.

You must be very careful here. The IRS is very picky about what constitutes an investment as opposed to a hobby. If you can clearly show that the purpose in acquiring the item was to make money—keeping items in their original packaging, purchasing insurance, perhaps—then you should not have any trouble.

Alternatively, if you sell your 1987 Toyota Camry and try to claim the difference between what you bought it for decades ago and what you sold it for in 2009, the IRS will take issue here. Claiming personal use property as a collectible will create some major tax headaches for you. So before you get cute about what you claim as a collectible investment, talk to a tax professional.

Real Estate Investment Losses

A few years back, anybody could buy a piece of real estate, sit on it for a week, and then turn around and sell it for a profit. This "easy money" led a lot of would-be moguls to sink their entire life savings into real estate just in time for the bubble to burst. If you're one of the thousands who lost their shirts in the real estate recession, there are ways to recover from your losses.

If you actively manage your properties, you may be able to claim a passive activity loss, which is deductible against passive activity gains. You didn't have any passive activity gains? The good news is that the losses never really go away. So, when the economy turns around and your properties start creating income for you, you can apply the built-up passive activity loss deductions to wipe out your future gains, even if it takes a decade or more to start making money again.

On the other hand, if you can't prove to the IRS that you are actively managing your properties and renting out the property, you may still be able to write off up to $25,000 in losses against ordinary income. If your adjusted gross income exceeds $150,000, you are not eligible to take the deduction.

That's all well and good for real estate you bought for investment purposes. But what if you had to sell your own home for a loss? Unfortunately, the IRS does not let you deduct losses on any personal use property, which is what it calls your primary residence. Even though your home is probably your biggest investment, the IRS does not allow you to claim losses for it.

On the other hand, if you sold your home for a significant profit, you may be on the hook for taxes. If you lived in the home for at least two out of the last five years, singles can exclude up to $250,000 worth of profits from income on a home sale—married couples can exclude up to $500,000 in profit. Any amount above that would be taxed at capital gains rates. Of course, if you were one of the lucky few to make a hefty profit on a home sale, remember, you can still offset the gains with capital losses!

Make a Charitable Gift of Stock

If you have appreciated stock that you've held for more than a year, and you plan to make significant charitable contributions before year-end, keep your cash and donate the stock (or mutual fund shares) instead. You'll avoid paying tax on the appreciation but will still be able to deduct the donated property's full value. If you want to maintain a position in the donated securities, you can immediately buy back shares. This idea works especially well with no-load mutual funds because there are no transaction fees involved.

However, if the stock is now worth less than when you acquired it, sell the stock, take the loss, and then give the cash to the charity. If you give the stock to the charity, your charitable deduction will equal the stock's current depressed value and no capital loss will be available. Also, if you sell the stock at a loss, you can't immediately buy back the shares as this will trigger the wash sale rules, which means your loss won't be deductible but instead will be added to the basis in the new shares.

Hardship Withdrawals

When the going gets tough, many people start taking what the IRS calls *hardship withdrawals* from their retirement plans. The IRS allows you to take these withdrawals for serious economic problems, like unemployment, illness, or injury. However, many retirement plans do not allow you take the withdrawals—check with your plan administrator before you attempt any withdrawals.

Unfortunately, even qualified hardship withdrawals are not immune from taxes. In addition to being taxed as ordinary income, the IRS will slap on a 10 percent early withdrawal penalty. Make sure there is no other way to make ends meet before you pull money out of your retirement savings.

Any Possibility of Borrowing?

Most retirement plans allow you to borrow up to $50,000 or 50 percent of the value of the account, whichever is less. This is penalty-free, unless you don't pay the money back, and then the usual early withdrawal penalties apply. This typically must be done within five years and definitely before changing employers. Employers, of course, have the option to make their plans' loan provisions more restrictive.

Although borrowing against your retirement plan may be an option, please note that it might not always be the best option. In fact, there are a whole host of negative consequences:

- Because you're borrowing the money, you'll need to pay back interest to your own 401(k) account at a competitive rate set by your plan administrator (usually the prime rate plus 2 percent).
- You are giving up the tax-free compounding of (1) the money you have in your retirement account that has been borrowed and (2) the money that will be used to pay back your loan. It can no longer be used to invest in the market and it no longer appreciates in value from interest, dividends, and other capital gains with the rest of your investment portfolio. That could lead to a significantly smaller nest egg come retirement.
- Your subsequent retirement savings may be curtailed—your plan may prevent you from continuing to fund your retirement until the loan is paid off or you may be subject to fees.
- The money used to pay back your loan is not tax-sheltered and may be another payroll deduction, reducing your take-home pay.

- Neither the loan nor the interest paid is tax-deductible—it is considered a consumer loan.
- If something happens and you need to give up your job or change employers, your loan will come immediately due (typically in sixty days) or run the risk of being treated as an early distribution—subject to taxation and early distribution penalties.
- If you do not make payments in accordance with the plan or IRS regulations, the outstanding loan balance will be declared in default. A defaulted loan, and possibly accrued interest on the loan balance, becomes a taxable distribution to the employee in the year of default with all the same tax penalties and implications of a withdrawal.
- It may permanently damage how you view your retirement account. Your retirement account should be a one-way street until actual retirement. If you fall into the trap of borrowing against your retirement account now, you will fall into the trap again and again. This diminishes the ability of your retirement account to grow unfettered.

Also note that a loan from a traditional IRA or Roth IRA is considered a prohibited transaction, and the IRS may disqualify your plan and tax you on the assets if you attempt it."

Sometimes people use the "sixty-day rollover" as a way to borrow funds temporarily from an IRA. Typically, a rollover is used to move IRA money between financial institutions. A distribution is made from the institution disbursing the funds. A check is then made payable directly to the participant. The participant has sixty days to make a rollover contribution to the receiving financial institution in order for the funds to retain their IRA status. This type of transaction can only be done once every twelve months with the same funds. The participant who receives the distribution will have that distribution reported to the IRS. Once the distribution is rolled into an IRA, the participant will be sent a Form 5498 to report on their taxes to nullify any tax consequence of the initial distribution.

As you can see, borrowing from your retirement requires a very high level of discipline to pull off without negative tax consequences. Thus, it is typically only recommended as a last resort.

The Death Tax

One of the biggest reasons people invest and grow their wealth is to leave a legacy for their children. We all want to pass a little something on to our loved ones after we pass, which is precisely why I hate estate taxes. The estate tax takes a huge chunk of your hard-earned savings right out of the hands of the people you intended to reward—your loved ones. I find it especially odious considering you already paid taxes on the funds when you earned them.

Here's the tricky thing: the future of the estate tax is an unknown. The Bush tax cuts of 2001 slowly reduced the estate tax until it was scheduled to disappear in 2010. The hope was that once it was gone, Congress would step in and make the estate tax repeal permanent. Sounds good, right?

Well, when the Great Recession hit and a Democratic Congress took over, most of us assumed that it would extend the 2009 estate tax rates indefinitely. That would have meant that estates exceeding $3.5 million—$7 million for married couples—would be taxed at a maximum of 45 percent. But then a strange thing happened; Congress closed its 2009 session without acting on the estate tax. The repeal was allowed to happen.

So, as 2010 began, there was no estate tax. Rumors abound that Congress will get around to reinstating it, and could even make it retroactive. This situation is creating an absolute nightmare for estate planning nationwide, not to mention the gallows humor surrounding the whole situation—jokes about helping rich Aunt Mildred pass on before the estate tax comes back. It's a little dark for my taste.

If Congress chooses to do nothing about the estate tax this year, hold on to your hat, because we are going back to the future in 2011. Seriously, the planned 2011 estate tax rates are those that were in place in 2001. This means that estates valued at more than $1 million will be taxed a maximum of 55 percent. Yikes!

Estate Planning

Regardless of what happens in Washington, creating an estate plan and keeping it updated is critical. I certainly have one, and so should anyone who wants to avoid the estate tax and family squabbles after he or she passes.

A smart plan uses tools ranging from life insurance to trusts to lower or even eliminate the estate tax and to prevent strife and bitter feuds among beneficiaries after a death. "Poor planning can destroy a family," says Les Kotzer, an attorney who wrote *Where There's an Inheritance—Stories from Inside the World of Two Wills Lawyers.* If no plan is in place or if terms are not explicitly spelled out, chaos can ensue, he says. Kotzer recalls a man who made a handwritten will leaving "all his personal stuff" to a son. A bitter court battle erupted as a daughter claimed "stuff" meant his power tools and personal possessions, not gold and diamond rings that their mother had owned. The son vowed to fight her to the gritty end, claiming he hoped his sister's legal fees would cost more than the jewelry was worth. I last heard that the UFC was in negotiation to televise their next Thanksgiving.

Don't let that happen to your family. These tips and tools can help you avoid such disasters:

- **Give Happily**—Let's start with a couple of simple techniques. For example, giving away money during your lifetime can reduce the value of your taxable estate. Here are the basics: You can give any number of individuals up to $13,000 each year without any tax consequences. If you choose to give more than $13,000 ($26,000 for married couples), you may be subject to the gift tax. You also have a tax credit that allows you to give up to $1 million during your lifetime without incurring taxes. In addition, there is no limit on how much you can give tax-free when you pay someone's higher education or medical expenses directly.

As far as how you make those gifts, you can simply hand a wad of cash to the recipient, but there are other choices. One popular method is a so-called Crummey trust, often used for children. This trust allows you to impose conditions on how and when the beneficiary gains access to the money. For example, many people choose to give their kids access to the funds in a trust when they turn twenty-one or upon completion of college.

- **Leverage Your Life Insurance**—If you're planning to leave property, a business, or other non-cash assets to your heirs, life insurance can be a lifesaver. If you purchase a policy that will cover the taxes on your estate, your heirs won't be faced with having to sell assets to pay the taxes. "Mom and Dad give money to the kids to take insurance out on their lives," says attorney Jeffrey Condon, author of *The Living Trust Advisor*. "When they die, the insurance company will write a check tax free to the kids." You can also set up a life insurance trust to be the beneficiary of the policy: that way, the death benefits won't be taxed as part of the estate.

- **Get Help**—Estate planning is a complicated affair. The help of a good financial advisor or an estate-planning attorney can make the entire ordeal much easier. And don't forget to find one with a complete understanding of the tax consequences of any plan drawn up.

Roni's Words of Wisdom

For my money, and no pun intended, we need more tax deductions for investing. Investing should be encouraged, and some tax breaks are a great way to motivate people, especially now when Americans can use all the financial help they can get.

Unfortunately for us, I don't believe the investment tax picture will improve anytime soon.

Our current administration is a little too keen on taxing investments. Take the capital gains tax—I am willing to bet that Washington politicians, looking to close the gap on deteriorating tax revenues, will place capital gains at the front of the line of potential tax hikes.

Doubling the capital gains tax rate was a primary plank of President Obama's campaign plan. The Obama administration wants to increase the capital gains tax rate from the current 15 percent to 28 percent. When taxes on investing go up, investing goes down.

Some would argue that there might be exceptions made for funds invested in small businesses. And that might be helpful to some, but more than anything I believe this will do very little for small business investors, further complicate an already overly complex tax system, and discourage investing overall.

I really get irked over hiking the capital gains tax rate because it's already a double tax. You paid taxes on your income when you earned it. Then you took that income and invested it. And when you cash in that investment, you pay taxes on that money again. Let's say you've put your after-tax dollars into a mutual fund for your retirement. After a few decades working, you might have $150,000 in those funds, $100,000 of which could be considered capital gains. Sounds great, right? Your investing paid off and you made some excellent earnings. Except that now you owe capital gains taxes on that $100,000.

With a capital gains rate at 15 percent, you would owe $15,000 in taxes. Unpleasant, isn't it? It gets worse; if the capital gains tax rate were raised to 28 percent, you would owe $28,000 in taxes. That extra $13,000 is nothing to sneeze at, and probably money you could very well use. But instead, good old Uncle Sam will take that, thank you very much.

But that's what happens when you have one group of politicians deciding that Wall Street is evil and must be taxed accordingly. It ends up punching the middle class in the gut. So, all you can do is learn everything you can about how investments are taxed and the deductions to which you might be entitled. Minimize the tax consequences and maximize the deduction savings. It's an education that pays for itself time and time again.

9

Behind on Your Tax Payments? Here's How to Negotiate Your Tax Bailout

Let us never negotiate out of fear. But let us never fear to negotiate.

—JOHN F. KENNEDY

The people who come to my law firm desperately seeking help with their tax problem share a lot of the same characteristics. Invariably, the person sitting across the desk is visibly anxious, sometimes in tears, with the body language of someone who just found out he or she has a terminal disease.

I'm an optimist. I also truly believe in the power of positive thinking. But I understand how hard it can be to stay upbeat when you're dealing with something as frightening and distressing as IRS debt. I hear about the sleepless nights, the stress, and the strain their relationships undergo during these trying times.

When faced with such a seemingly overwhelming problem, the person across the desk needs some comfort. He or she needs to hear that the world is not going to end, that this is the low point, that everything from here on out is going to get to better. Once these innocent taxpayers see that there are solutions, they begin to relax, smile a little, and get back to sleep at night.

I love to see the glimmer of hope that appears in clients' eyes when they realize that they will be getting bailed out of their tax problems—something they didn't think was possible.

Negotiating with the IRS is possible, but it isn't easy. Make no mistake; there is no magic wand that will make your tax problems disappear. The process can be long and about as pleasant as going twelve rounds with a hungry grizzly bear. The IRS makes the rules and changes them whenever it suits it.

So, with all this stacked against you, how can you possibly come out on top? In my experience, the best weapon to defeat the IRS collection machine is usually your own financial situation. For example, if the real estate bust left you with no equity in your home, bereft of any meaningful savings, investments, and assets and unlikely to see any wage increases in the near future, the IRS may settle your entire debt for a small amount of money. The whole idea is to prove that what paltry assets you have are not worth the cost of seizing them.

Of course, if the IRS is convinced that your hard times are only temporary and that you have some assets worth collecting, it won't be as willing to settle for peanuts.

Remember, in negotiating with the IRS, it's not about how much you owe. It's about how much you can pay. And you are not steering those IRS negotiations—the IRS is driving. However, with a little more knowledge and a better understanding of the IRS collection process, you can swing the negotiations back in your favor.

IRS Negotiations: Seven Stages of Tax Grief

Living with IRS debt is awful. I've heard it compared to a root canal, spending the day at the DMV, and even a long weekend in Newark.

But *negotiating* with the IRS can be even worse if you don't know the tricks of the trade.

In all my years of representing clients with tax debts, I've learned that no one wants to end up on the wrong side of the IRS. Usually the debt is a result of a job loss, medical problem, or any number of personal calamities. The reasons vary, but the process is often the same.

It usually starts with an ominous letter in your mailbox—a terse note informing you that you owe the IRS money. Big money.

That feeling of panic you get from reading the notice is one I wouldn't wish on my worst enemy. In fact, I've often said that being in debt to the IRS is a life-altering experience. Those who have been through it can attest that the entire debt and negotiation process is akin to the seven stages of grief.

Stage 1: Shock and Denial—'You just ripped open the letter from the IRS and you've read the contents. You're in disbelief. You might even deny the reality of the situation in order to avoid the pain. Therapists say that shock fuels wave after wave of emotional protection to keep you from being overwhelmed all at once. But eventually the information sinks in, leading directly to Stage 2.

Stage 2: Pain and Guilt—As the shock abates, it is replaced by waves of pain and guilt. Yes, actual pain, as though someone just punched you in the gut. The guilt and shame emerge as you examine what horrible things you must have done to be in such a situation. Try to remember, even when you're in the throes of Stage 2, you are not a bad person; you were just unfortunate enough to fall prey to the IRS.

Stage 3: Anger and Bargaining—Eventually pain and guilt give way to anger. You may find yourself lashing out and laying the blame for your tax troubles on someone else, like your accountant, employer, or spouse. More often than not, I have found this exercise to be fruitless. No matter what happened previously, it's your name on the IRS notice. Blaming others will not make them responsible for the debts in the eyes of the IRS. Instead, it distracts you from what must be done now. My advice is to blow off that steam in a healthy way, at the gym or with a run through the park.

Stage 4: Depression, Reflection, Loneliness—Once the anger subsides comes the sadness. At a time when you really need to be creating a plan to fight back, you might be feeling down in the dumps, obsessing over how this could have happened, lamenting your tax plight. Try to use this overly analytical mood to motivate you toward action. Talk it out with a tax professional and gain comfort in taking some positive action.

Stage 5: The Rebound—Once you've moved on past depression and reflection and hopefully on to meaningful action, you'll begin to feel a lift in your spirits. You start to see a way out, far off though it may be. As you move toward a plan for dealing with your tax troubles, you'll start to reclaim your sense of normalcy and all the good things that come with it. You'll smile back at people, perhaps laugh a little easier. In my experience, this stage usually sets in as you take action on your tax debt resolution plan.

Stage 6: Reconstruction—As you make headway on your road to resolution, your mood will improve as your plan gains momentum and starts to bear fruit. Perhaps you've even successfully negotiated a resolution with the IRS. You can see the light at the end of the tunnel, and you begin to feel confident that your plan is actually working.

Stage 7: Acceptance and Hope—Once your resolution is accepted by the IRS, you find yourself looking forward to the future. You can view the entire IRS ordeal as a learning experience, and you can look at yourself in the mirror and like the person you see again. As I've said, there are few sweeter moments than beating back the IRS and learning to love life again. It's a feeling I hope you get after reading this book—and in learning to give the taxman a dose of his own medicine.

Step-by-Step Guide to Resolving a Tax Debt

Okay, my "Seven Stages of Tax Grief" is a quick overview of the emotional and psychological impact of an IRS tax problem.

Now you need to know what action must be taken to get out of this thing with the least amount of damage to your wallet, your life, and your sense of well-being. Let's take this time to analyze your step-by-step moves when the IRS comes calling, looking for your hard-earned cash.

Quick Tips When You Find Out You Owe the IRS

- *Don't* put the letters in a drawer and hope they will go away.
- If it's a "demand" (that you pay) letter, respond to the letter right away.
- Contact a tax specialist! Getting help quickly can mean the difference between success and failure and potentially thousands and thousands of dollars.
- Consider a payment plan. Once the IRS agrees to a settlement plan, the IRS ceases all collection action, stops seizures of your cars, home, or garnishment of your wages and/or bank account, and the interest and penalties stop accruing.
- Make the payments. If an emergency occurs, making a payment impossible, contact the IRS immediately and work out an alternate arrangement.

Step 1: Communicate right now. The worst thing you can do is ignore the problem. Never put off contacting the IRS when a notice arrives or you get a phone call. The longer you wait and procrastinate, the nastier the penalties become. Get your wits about you and get on the phone. You do not need to agree to anything at this point. In fact, my recommendation is not to give up any information at all. Instead, simply call to acknowledge you received the notice, verify the balances due, confirm all returns have been filed, and ask for more time to respond.

It may seem useless to call without a plan in mind, but you may even find a more compassionate ear from the IRS because of your forthright attitude. I know it's unpleasant, but trust me, you'll survive. Just remember, do not agree to anything the IRS says at this point in the game. You are solely opening the lines of communication and confirming relevant information while asking for additional time to respond.

Step 2: Contact a reputable tax specialist. After opening the lines of communication, you should immediately consult with professional help. If you have an accountant with whom you are comfortable and you are confident of his or her work, that's excellent. If not, you need to get a move on! Ask your friends; thumb through the phone book. You need to find someone with experience negotiating with the IRS and a proven track record of ethical behavior and professional conduct. And you need to find that person fast. Interest and penalties will continue to accrue, so the longer you wait, the bigger your debt becomes.

Step 3: Compliance. At this point, either you or your hired tax professional need to verify your compliance. This means checking to see that all required tax returns have been filed and that all current year tax obligations (e.g., withholding taxes, estimated taxes, payroll taxes, etc.) are paid. This means you may need to file a past-due tax return when you find out the IRS believes you had enough income in a past year to require a return. It means you may have to go to your payroll office to adjust your withholdings. Finally, in doing your compliance research, get updated past-due amounts for each tax year and the date in which the tax debt will expire (i.e., Collection Statute Expiration Date) if the debt is six years or older.

Step 4: Review your financial situation. Once compliance is confirmed, either you or your tax professional needs to review your financial situation to determine the appropriate type of tax debt resolution program. If going on your own, you will need to complete your financial statements (Forms 433-A and 433-B, Collection Information Statements) to determine your available income and asset value, as well as for negotiating with the IRS. Completing the forms will help you find the type of resolution for which you qualify. Alternatively, many tax professionals offer free and confidential tax debt analysis in order to make this determination. They will then transfer the relevant data to the forms after you hire them to represent you.

Step 5: Try to work out a resolution. As you will learn, the Offer in Compromise (OIC) is the holy grail of tax settlements. But remember, the IRS only agrees to a resolution if it believes it's the best possible outcome for the agency, and the requirements for qualifying for an OIC leave many taxpayers ineligible. So, if an OIC is not in the cards for you, your next option is to work out an Installment Agreement. This is essentially a payment plan, wherein you will repay the total debt, plus interest and penalties, over several years. When you submit a request to the IRS for an Installment Agreement, you will have a better chance of success if you:

- Let the IRS know that you plan to pay off your debt but are limited by your financial situation.

- Have the help of a reputable tax professional on your side, one who has experience negotiating with the IRS and can figure out what you can afford to pay.
- Commit to paying the IRS on a regular basis until the debt is paid off. If you fail to do so, the IRS may slap you with a lien to collect the rest.

If your financial situation does not allow you to make any type of payment at all toward satisfying your back tax debt, then you may be eligible for placement on the IRS's Currently Not Collectible status. I will discuss this in further detail later on in this chapter.

Step 6: Stick to your plan. Once you reach a workable solution for your tax debt, above all else, stick to it! The IRS will not hold back if you miss a payment or violate the terms of your arrangement in any way. Instead, it will be back to slap you with liens, levies, even property seizures. And this time, it won't be so willing to enter into a resolution. If life throws you a curve ball, get back in touch with the IRS to make alternate arrangements before you miss a payment.

Conditions for an Offer in Compromise

The IRS doesn't exactly shout this news out to the world, but it will settle tax debts for less than you owe—if you meet any of the following criteria:

- Doubt as to Liability—Meaning the IRS is not 100 percent certain that the debt it has assessed is correct.
- Doubt as to Collectability—There is no question as to the amount owed, but the IRS doubts you could ever pay the full amount of tax assessed. This is the most common form of OIC.

- Effective Tax Administration—The amount owed is correct, and the IRS believes it could collect the amount owed, but an exceptional circumstance exists that allows the IRS to consider a settlement. Generally, this involves proving that paying the tax debt in full would create an overwhelming economic hardship or would be unfair and inequitable. Historically, this is the most rarely accepted form of OIC.

When the IRS settles a debt for less than the amount owed, it is called an Offer in Compromise (OIC). In order to be considered for an OIC, a taxpayer must have met all of the following requirements:

- Filed the most current version of Form 656, Offer in Compromise, and Forms 433-A and 433-B, Collection Information Statement;
- Submitted the $150 application fee, or Form 656-A, Income Certification for Offer in Compromise Application Fee, with the Form 656;
- Filed all required federal tax returns;
- If you are an employer, you must have filed and paid any required employment tax returns on time for the two quarters prior to filing the OIC, and you must be current with deposits for the quarter in which the OIC was submitted; and
- Must not be a debtor in a bankruptcy case.

The IRS lays out some examples of tax cases that could be settled. These include:

- Taxpayer is incapable of earning a living because of a long-term illness, medical condition, or disability and it is reasonably foreseeable that taxpayer's financial resources will be exhausted providing for care and support during the course of the condition;

- Although taxpayer has certain assets, liquidation of those assets to pay outstanding tax liabilities would render the taxpayer unable to meet basic living expenses; and
- Although taxpayer has certain assets, the taxpayer is unable to borrow against the equity in those assets and disposition by seizure or sale of the assets would have sufficient adverse consequences such that enforced collection is unlikely.

Negotiating with the IRS: In Compromise

As I already mentioned, the IRS has several ways of resolving a tax debt. The OIC program can be an incredible resolution if you qualify.

Therein lies the difficulty. The IRS will only settle for less than the total amount if it's in its best interest. This is determined by reviewing your financial situation, which you will lay out using IRS Forms 656 and 433 (small businesses would use Form 433-B). These forms tally up the total value of your assets, including your home. It also compares all sources of your income to all allowable monthly expenses. Filling out this form is the monetary equivalent to a full physical, and can leave you feeling just as exposed.

Extra Conditions Attached to an Offer in Compromise

The IRS also adds that, besides other conditions, the taxpayer has to agree that he or she will file and pay all their taxes for a period of five years after the offer. If not, Uncle Sam has the right to rescind the compromise agreement.

Source: Internal Revenue Service

The forms will also determine what your OIC amount actually is. You can either fill out the forms on your own or with the help of a tax professional. Once you complete and file the forms and hand over the $150 application fee (non-refundable, of course), IRS staffers get into the act. An IRS representative will review your information and decide whether to accept your original offer. If not, the IRS can opt to calculate a different offer amount and tell you that's what it is willing to accept.

Be careful when completing any negotiation forms with the IRS. If your paperwork is incomplete or if you don't meet specific deadlines, the IRS can reject your application. Also, adhere to the deadline included in the application forms. Any missing documentation or information will result in a rejected offer, though the IRS will keep the application fee, thank you.

You may need to make a payment toward your final OIC when you apply. As of 2010, the IRS requires that any OIC filing include a payment totaling 20 percent of the total offer amount. So, if your offer is for $20,000 on a $100,000 back tax debt, you would need to send your application with a payment of $4,000 to be considered for an OIC. This payment is non-refundable, even if the IRS rejects your offer. Instead, the IRS will keep the funds and apply it toward your debt.

When and if the IRS agrees to a payoff amount, the agency will accept the OIC. Once that happens, the IRS will stop any collection activity and start working on payment arrangements. By and large, most OICs wind up as lump sum settlements where the taxpayer agrees to settle up with the government in no more than five payments, and usually in no later than ninety days.

If coming up with a large sum of cash on a few months' notice is outside your ability, you certainly aren't alone. Nor are you without other options. Offers in Compromise are not suitable for everyone. So, don't be afraid to look at other options, like an Installment Agreement or placement on the Currently Not Collectible status.

Reasons to Hire a Tax Professional

Cutting a deal with the IRS is not just difficult; it can also be painful. To alleviate some of the pain and reduce a lot of your stress, get an experienced tax professional, one who can negotiate with the IRS on your behalf. Let them deal with the countless hours of back and forth with the IRS, with waiting on hold for hours at a time, with the frustration of IRS computer "errors."

Need even more reasons?

1. **Experience**—Tax professionals, especially those with several years working in the trenches against the IRS, are good partners to have in your corner when you square off against the government. A smart tax professional knows the IRS's tortuous tax code like the back of his or her hand.

2. **A Strong Advocate**—Hey, it's no secret that IRS agents can be bulldogs when they're owed back taxes. If you're in the IRS's crosshairs, then why not have a bulldog of your own? You'd be surprised how fast the IRS backs down when you have an advocate who knows the tax rules better than the IRS does and isn't afraid to show it.

3. **No Loose Lips**—You might spill some information that the IRS does not need to know when dealing with a tax professional. Not to worry; a good, ethical tax specialist will keep those conversations private. Tax advocates who want to stay in business don't make much of a living if they share your private conversations with the IRS.

4. **Master Negotiators**—I've sat across the table from a lot of IRS agents in my day, and I can tell you firsthand that a good negotiator can make an agent melt faster than a pat of butter in a hot skillet. A savvy, seasoned tax professional can broker a favorable tax resolution for you because he or she speaks the same language as the IRS agent.

5. **A Level Playing Field**—As I've already said in this book, the IRS intimidates a lot of our clients. I completely understand, given the IRS's overbearing history. But a good tax specialist won't back down from even the toughest IRS agent because he or she knows what the agent knows. Once the playing field has been leveled, negotiations usually go a lot smoother.

Negotiating with the IRS: Installment Agreement

As I mentioned earlier, Installment Agreements (IA) are the usual mechanism for making regular, agreed-upon payments. Such payments allow for the full payment of the tax debt in smaller, more manageable amounts. Just make sure you know the rules going into the resolution. In order to qualify for an IA with the IRS, you must clear some hurdles:

- You must have filed all required tax returns. You may have outstanding debts on those returns, but the returns must be filed.
- You must disclose all of your assets, including all investments and bank accounts.
- If you have enough cash to satisfy your debt in your checking, savings, money market, and/or brokerage account, you must use the cash to resolve the debt. If you've got the funds, you can't decide *not* to use them.
- If you can borrow from the equity in your home, the IRS will want to know that, too. It may even insist that you take out a home equity loan to satisfy your IRS debts.
- You must complete the personal financial statement. If your business is involved in the tax debt, you will need to complete a business financial statement.

- Installment agreement payments are almost always determined by your total monthly income less your allowable monthly expenses—such as housing, transportation, grocery, and medical expenses.

Keep in mind that just like most debt repayment plans, interest on your tax debt will continue to accrue until the entire liability is repaid.

Watch Out for Scams

I love my profession, and most people in this industry are ethical professionals. However, there are always those scammers looking to make a buck off of your misfortune.

Some are people claiming to be former IRS employees who know the "inside scoop," guaranteeing they can settle your debt. The worst part is that good people get suckered into the sales pitch and end up paying through the nose for empty promises.

Remember, everyone's financial situation is different, so even if the guy on the commercial swears that his tax debt was wiped out, it doesn't mean you will have the same experience.

So, how do you tell the scammers from the legitimate, ethical professionals? Well, first realize that if it sounds too good to be true, then it probably is. Keep a keen ear out for promises they cannot possibly keep. For example, if someone swears up and down that they can get your OIC accepted, but they've never even asked about your financial situation, then you should be wary—very wary.

Finally, when in doubt, you can call the local IRS office to ask about a particular professional or company. The people there should be able to tell you whether or not the professional is able to represent a taxpayer before the IRS.

Negotiating with the IRS: Currently Not Collectible

In this crummy economic climate, more and more average people are finding themselves unable to pay for even the most basic needs. And for people like this, a surprise tax debt can be enough to drive them over the edge.

If you're one of the millions struggling just to get by, you need to know about the Currently Not Collectible (CNC) status. CNC status protects a taxpayer from IRS collection activity while the statute of limitations on the debt continues to run. Why would the IRS agree to stop collection actions without a repayment agreement?

The IRS might be soulless, but it isn't completely irrational. When you apply for placement on CNC status, you disclose to the IRS your complete financial picture. So, if you do not own anything of value, and all your income goes to pay the most basic of expenses (like rent, groceries, and medical costs), the IRS can see, clear as day, that collection efforts against you will be fruitless. The agents realize that the amount of time and energy they put into coming after you is not worth what they can hope to collect. So, instead, they back off, hoping to give you time to get your life and your finances in order.

Once your circumstances improve, through a better economy or a better job perhaps, the IRS can revisit your tax debt and arrange for repayment.

Now, a lot of people are thinking, what if your situation doesn't improve? Although CNC status is designed to be a temporary respite from IRS collections, it is entirely possible for you to stay on CNC status until your debt expires (more on expiring tax debts later). And oftentimes, for taxpayers on fixed incomes (e.g., Social Security, pensions, disability), that is exactly what occurs.

The steps for placement on CNC status are very similar to those for an IA:

- You must disclose to the IRS your financial situation by filing Form 433.
- If Form 433 shows that your monthly expenses exceed your monthly income, you may qualify for placement on CNC status.
- You must be current on all your tax return filings. You may owe back taxes on the returns; the returns just must be filed.
- Once the IRS has received your completed Form 433, the negotiating begins.
- Either on the phone or in writing, you will need to request placement on CNC status. The IRS may require further proof of your finances such as bank statements, pay stubs, etc.
- Once the IRS is satisfied that you are unable to make a payment of any kind toward your debt, you will be placed on CNC status and all collection activity should stop.

Although CNC status will save you from active collections, any liens placed on your property will remain in place until the debt is paid or expires. So, although CNC can save you from having your wages garnished, by no means is it a get-out-of-jail-free card.

Do You Qualify for Hardship Status?

In this tough economy, the IRS is fielding more and more calls from taxpayers asking for leniency due to financial hardship.

All that means is that if you can prove a true hardship—such as a job loss or catastrophic medical problem—the IRS will work with you to cease collection efforts temporarily. This can allow you just enough breathing room to get back on your feet and keep your family financially afloat.

Negotiating with the IRS: Waiting It Out

IRS tax debts do not live forever. The IRS has ten years from the date the tax was assessed to collect from you. This is called the statute of limitations, and once that date passes, you are no longer obligated to pay your tax debt. So, if you have a particularly old debt and IRS collection activities are not breaking your back, you may be able to just hang on a little longer and let the debt expire.

Of course, this will not work for everyone and the IRS has some sneaky ways of extending the statute of limitations on your debt. For example, a bankruptcy filing can extend the statute of limitations. Sometimes the IRS will ask you to sign a waiver, extending the expiration date as a condition of entering into a settlement (though you are not in any way legally obligated to sign such a document). So, before you crumple up those IRS notices and hunker down for a long wait, you should verify that the debt is actually set to expire when you think it does. The easiest way to do this is to request a copy of your tax accounts from the IRS and carefully review the information contained with a tax professional. Alternatively, have your tax professional ask for the Collection Statute Expiration Date.

If the dates are all correct and your life isn't being negatively impacted by IRS collection activity, you might be able to get out from under that debt without having to part with your hard-earned cash.

Negotiating with the IRS: Bankruptcy

I discussed bankruptcy at length earlier in chapter 7, so you already know that filing for bankruptcy can resolve some tax debts. Of course, there are myriad consequences, both financial and personal, of filing for bankruptcy. But for those with a number of outstanding debts including tax debt, it can be the fresh start they so desperately need.

A number of factors must be considered before back taxes can be discharged in bankruptcy. First, you need to qualify for bankruptcy. Second, you need to file the bankruptcy properly. Third, you need to examine the age and type of back taxes. In general, recently assessed federal income taxes cannot be discharged in bankruptcy. Additionally, business-related federal payroll back taxes generally cannot be discharged in bankruptcy.

If you are considering filing for bankruptcy, take my advice and get a bankruptcy attorney to show you the ropes.

Your Rights

The IRS is the ultimate creditor. It has dozens of special rights when it comes to collecting past-due taxes on behalf of the federal government. These special rights account for the multiple and aggressive collection techniques the IRS has at its disposal.

However, taxpayers have their own respective rights. It is important to understand these rights if you owe back taxes to the IRS. To stay prepared, please enjoy the following list of the top seven taxpayer debt collection rights.

1. **Representation**—First and foremost, you have the right to represent yourself before the IRS to dispute any unpaid taxes or additional fees. Alternatively, you have the right to seek help from a professional to represent you before the IRS. However, your representative must be a person allowed to practice before the IRS, such as a tax attorney, certified public accountant, or IRS enrolled agent.

2. **Protection of Rights**—According to the IRS's code, all employees must explain and protect your rights throughout all contacts and negotiations.

Self-Employed? You're More Likely to Owe Back Taxes

Millions of people across the United States currently owe the IRS back taxes. What do a majority of these people have in common? They are self-employed.

Although wage-earning employees usually have taxes automatically withheld from their pay, self-employed people do not have such a safety net. That means these entrepreneurial folks must be very disciplined and organized to make sure all their required taxes,

3. **Confidentiality**—The IRS is not allowed to disclose information you give to the IRS to anyone, except as authorized by law. Additionally, you have the right to know how the information will be used and what happens if the requested information is not provided.

4. **Records of Contacts**—Although the IRS is allowed to contact third parties about your IRS debt without your consent, you do have the right to request a list of all the people contacted.

5. **Meeting Companion**—Taxpayers also have the right to have someone accompany them during interviews with IRS representatives. You can even make audio recordings of any meetings for your records.

6. **Good Faith**—If you can show that you acted reasonably and in good faith and/or relied on bad advice from an IRS representative, you have the right to request that all penalties assessed by the IRS be waived.

7. **IRS Appeals Office**—If you disagree with the IRS on the amount of the tax liability or collection actions taken by the IRS, you even have the right to ask a court or the IRS Appeals Office to review the case.

including self-employment taxes, are paid regularly throughout the year, through estimated tax payments.

If you earn money that does not have taxes automatically withheld, make sure you understand the tax obligations that come along with being self-employed. A little extra attention to your taxes will save you from tangling with the taxman later on.

Potential Problems in Talking with the IRS

What a shocker—dealing with the IRS comes with some inherent problems. One way or another, it seems the IRS is bound and determined to get your goat. To prepare you for battle, you need to be aware of some of the issues that often arise when working directly with the IRS and what to do about them.

SURPRISE VISITS

By law, an IRS representative can show up at your home or place of business to confront you about your back tax liability.

If you get a knock on the door from the cold fist of the IRS, answer it and immediately request the IRS representative's identification number and contact information. From there, let the IRS agent know that you have hired representation for your tax problem and that he or she needs to communicate with your representative directly. You are not obligated to answer the agent's questions, so politely terminate the visit and immediately call your tax professional.

LOST IN THE MAIL

What is it about one federal agency, the IRS, regularly losing your tax forms, and then blaming it on another federal agency, the U.S. Postal Service? After all, can't two federal government agencies get along? But that's Uncle Sam's version of *The Odd Couple* for you. The IRS does a bulk of its communicating via snail mail, and darned if it doesn't have the worst track record for getting things through the post office.

To cover your behind, anything you send to the IRS should be sent using certified mail, with a delivery receipt requested.

If you have hired a representative for your tax case, make sure you send him or her copies of every IRS notice and letter you receive. The IRS should be sending copies to your rep as well, but again, it has a terrible track record with the post office. It's always better to cover your bases and send copies.

DROWNING IN DOCUMENTATION

Death by paperwork is one of the IRS's favorite tactics. In fact, one of the most frustrating aspects of dealing with the IRS is responding to multiple document requests. Before the IRS will accept any forms showing your financial situation, it requires that you substantiate your income, expenses, and assets by providing written proof of each. Unfortunately, that's just the nature of the beast.

To mitigate this headache, prepare beforehand. Get your financial documents organized, and start collecting every financial document you can get your hands on: pay stubs, bank statements, loan documents, receipts for expenses . . . everything. No matter what, do *not* send the IRS the original documents—ever. Make copies and send those. The IRS is notorious for losing documents but will not give you a break because it loses your documents.

ON HOLD CLASSICAL MUSIC

Roll over, Beethoven. If you have ever called the IRS, you know that it loves its classical music. You probably also know that the IRS has a very limited collection, because the same tunes seem to rotate over and over again. And with IRS wait times being what they are, you probably know these tunes by heart.

Those wait times are simply the result of being "extremely busy," or so claims the IRS. But there isn't much you can do about it. So, before you call, be prepared with some crossword puzzles or some mundane tasks to keep you occupied while you wait. And bring a boatload of patience to get you through the ninth repetition of "Für Elise."

IRS COMPUTER FAILURES

Why is it that, just when you start making some progress in your negotiation, the IRS computers will inevitably crash, forcing you to call back another time? And darned if the notes from your previous call aren't missing from the files.

Believe it or not, the "computer ate our homework" excuse is an intentional one. My experience is that these computer failures really only seem to occur when the case starts to go the taxpayer's way. Again, there is not much you can do—heck, the IRS does it to the attorneys at my law firm all of the time. You may be helped by keeping your own call notes, including the date and time of the call and the ID number for the IRS representative to whom you spoke.

MASSIVE CONFUSION

Bureaucracy, thy name is the IRS. No matter how many times you call or how many people you speak with, it seems the IRS just can't ever decide who has been assigned to your account or the status of your case. Is it sitting with Collections? Assigned to a Revenue Officer? Who knows? Without fail, you'll be passed from department to department without making any headway at all. It's hell on earth, all brought to you by the powers that be at the IRS.

Here, once again, is where a smart, experienced tax specialist can help. A good tax professional is trained to track down who he or she needs to deal with in order to resolve your tax liability. So, buck up. All you have to do is remain patient while your representative jumps through hoops for you to try to get you the tax resolution you deserve.

Roni's Words of Wisdom—Tips for Working Effectively with a Tax Professional

Just hiring a tax professional does not ensure a successful resolution. No, you must take an active role in your tax case, making sure to fulfill your responsibilities so your tax professional can fulfill his or hers. Here is what you need to do to give your case the highest chance of success:

1. **Respond quickly to all letters and phone calls.** This is the first item because it is the most important one. Your tax specialist will need to communicate with you often throughout the life of your case, via phone, fax, and snail mail. It is crucial that you respond as quickly as possible to any type of communication sent your way. Delays in your response will delay your case!

2. **Save all your financial documents.** You already know that any IRS negotiation is based on your current financial situation. So, the IRS will require proof of your situation in the form of pay stubs, bank statements, receipts, and proof of payment for expenses. By starting to save it all now, you'll be sure to have anything the IRS requires ready to go.

3. **Pay your taxes.** If you are a wage-earning employee, your tax professional may ask you to adjust your withholding to make sure you are not creating another hefty tax bill next year. Of course, if you're on course for a refund, your tax professional might ask you to reduce your withholding because the IRS will keep your refund and apply it toward your debt.

    On the other hand, if you are self-employed, your tax professional will ask you to start making your estimated quarterly tax payments. This is to ensure you are fully compliant with all your tax obligations as required by the IRS.

Although "pay your taxes" may not sound like sexy advice, it is doubly beneficial. Not only does it bring you into compliance, but it increases the amount of allowable expenses your tax professional can claim for purposes of negotiating a resolution to your tax debt.

4. **Don't hide assets or income.** Your tax professional cannot be a party to you illegally transferring or hiding any assets or income. If he or she discovers any illegal dealings on your part, ethical and professional rules may demand terminating your representation.

5. **Don't contact the IRS on your own.** Progress may seem slow for a while, which may lead you to wonder, "What's going on?" But before you start dialing Uncle Sam to see what's up, stop. You hired a tax professional to negotiate with the IRS for you. If you call the IRS on your own, you could jeopardize your tax case and undo any progress your representative has made. If you have questions about where your case is or what progress is being made, your best bet is to request a meeting or conference call with your representative.

10

State Tax Issues, State Tax Bailout Options

All politics is local.

—THOMAS P. O'NEILL

As perilous as our federal government's economic situation is, it is nothing compared to most states' problems. In my home state of California, our fiscal situation is so out of control that the governor has taken to issuing IOUs in lieu of paychecks and threatening to keep tax refunds! Suffice it to say, most states are a complete mess.

Through mid-2009 (in the midst of one of the most historic and brutal economic downturns in U.S. history), state tax revenues plummeted 11.7 percent—the sharpest decline in forty-six years, according to a report by the Rockefeller Institute of Government. Overall, forty-five of the fifty states experienced revenue dropoffs. Like any government entity with budget problems, just guess where state governments are turning to get their cash bailout? From you, of course.

States' "Rights"

When the heat is on taxpayers, much of the focus and energy centers on accommodating the voracious tax needs of Uncle Sam. People often forget about their state tax obligations. But anyone who has tangled with tax problems can attest that although dealing with the IRS is a nightmare, it's nothing compared to dealing with state tax boards.

You just can't afford to forget that the state you live in also collects taxes. As the preceding statistics indicate, most states are in pretty bad shape and are aggressively looking for ways to balance their bloated budgets. Although the federal government may be bailing out the banks and big businesses, it hasn't had the resources to deal with states that are over budget and short on cash.

Certainly, the stimulus package was supposed to help states stay fiscally afloat. However, the funds were extremely limited, and once the money was spent, there wasn't another check in the mail.

Take my home state of California. They may call it the Golden State, but the state bank account is anything but golden. In 2009, a magnificent $27 billion dollar budget deficit kept the state from fulfilling its payroll obligations. Granted, California is the most populous state in the nation, so it stands to reason that it would have bigger budget problems than say Wyoming or Vermont, but the solution wasn't a pretty one. In addition to a cut of $15 billion for services from the state budget, residents have also been hit with a 0.25 percent increase in income tax. State employees have the added burden of mandatory unpaid furlough days and pay cuts. Even so, California has billions to make up before it's solvent—if it ever gets there. Therefore, California's governor, faced with a state battered by the recession and a $42 billion deficit last winter, proposed new taxes on everything from alcohol to veterinary services. He ultimately signed $12.5 billion in temporary tax hikes on income, sales, and vehicles, the last of which was the very tax he came to Sacramento to reduce. The governor defended his switch by saying the historic downturn had become so severe that California had "a revenue problem rather than a spending problem."

That's just one state's problems, and California certainly isn't the only hard-up state. Other states are finding ways to increase revenue by slipping their hands into your wallets as well. In Wisconsin, they've extended the sales tax on entertainment to items such as subscriptions to magazines and music downloads. If you bought a hybrid vehicle and live in the state of Washington, you used to get a tax exemption. Not anymore; it's been eliminated. And it will cost you more to enjoy wine or beer in New York since the state raised the sales tax on those items. In Pennsylvania, state government is considering a 16 percent tax increase to help balance its budget.

With the crushing recession impacting every state in the nation and every type of business, it stands to reason that fewer taxes are being collected in every category, including property tax, income, and sales tax.

Because the federal government isn't bailing out individual states, the states are looking to you and me to bail them out. Throughout 2009, many states either raised taxes or had proposals in the works to raise taxes. Most states collect not only income tax but also business tax, sales tax, and, of course, property tax through local municipalities. These taxes account for a majority of each state's revenue. With less money coming through these existing taxes, you can bet that you'll see higher state taxes and new taxes across these great United States.

Fifty Powder Kegs

The ongoing decline in tax receipts has triggered huge state budget problems. In 2009, forty-eight states addressed shortfalls in their budgets—a number totaling $166 billion, or 24 percent of state budgets. New data shows a majority of states expect shortfalls in 2010 and 2011 as well. Aggregate gaps through 2011 likely will exceed $350 billion.

Steps to Take if You're Behind on Your State Taxes

Every state is an island unto itself. As such, there is no single, uniform way that states collect taxes or work with taxpayers to resolve tax debts.

Each has its own legislature, its own constitution, and its own method of financing public services that may lean on income taxes a lot (like Massachusetts and New Jersey) or not at all (like New Hampshire or Florida).

Currently, forty-one states collect individual income taxes, and thirty-five of those states use the federal tax system as a blueprint for collecting their own taxes. In a nutshell, that means the steps you use to pay a federal tax return (collecting financial records, hiring a tax advisor, and sending your tax returns in, either via mail or online) are the same steps you'll use to pay your state taxes.

By extension, if you owe back taxes, you'll likely repay them the same way you do your federal taxes—just sent to a different office. So, when you get a notice of back tax liabilities from your state tax board, you'll find that some action steps are universal. Let's take a look at some concrete moves we can make to keep state tax officials off our collective backs.

1. **Get your records in order.** If you need to file state back taxes, you'll likely need to dig up copies of old tax records (things like W-2 forms and 1099 forms). Your employer should have copies of your old W-2s, but that's not guaranteed (businesses aren't obligated to hang on to employee tax forms for a long period of time). You are always better off keeping your own forms filed away in a safe deposit box or a secure location in your home.

2. **Collect your state tax forms.** Make sure you have all your state tax forms in order. If you find you are missing anything, visit your state tax board's website to find out how to get blank copies. The website may also have useful information on your state's practices for collecting back taxes. (See chapter 12 to find your state's tax office website.)

3. **Reach out and touch the state tax revenue office.** Just like when dealing with a federal debt, you must be proactive and reach out to your state tax board. Make the call, and find out your state's specific resolution options and how to start the process. You may also get the information you need by visiting your state revenue office's website. Remember, the more forthright you are with those in the tax office, the more likely they will be to work with you on a resolution. The fastest path to a lien on your home or a wage garnishment judgment is to do nothing and hope that your back taxes obligation goes away by itself. With states starving for cash, that's not a very likely option.

4. **Review your options.** If you owe money, they'll be coming after you; it's just a matter of time. Many states have resolution options that mirror the federal options I explained in chapter 9. A few of the more common state tax resolution methods are:

   - **Installment Agreement**—Under an installment payment plan, you submit monthly payments to cover your state back taxes that, over time, will pay off your debt, ideally without significantly impacting your lifestyle.
   - **Offer in Compromise**—An Offer in Compromise program provides taxpayers who owe the state more than they could ever afford to pay the opportunity to resolve their entire debt for a lesser payment.

- **Tax Amnesty**—In this situation, the state creates a limited window of time during which the state will reduce or remove penalties, allowing those with tax debts to come forward to pay off the liabilities without additional fees. The aim is to recoup as much money as possible.
- **Consumer Credit Counseling Service**—Usually, this is a not-for-profit agency that can help you straighten out your finances, reduce total debts, and plan a tax repayment strategy. Check with your state tax board to find a reputable organization.

5. **Make a plan and stick to it.** Once your state tax board agrees to a resolution, stick to the plan! Remember, states also have the ability to garnish your wages, levy your bank accounts, and put liens on your property.

State Tax Resolution Methods

I've listed the most common methods of state tax resolution in the previous section. Remember, every state runs its own tax system, and other options may be available to you. On the other hand, even if your state offers one of the preceding options, the rules governing the program may be completely different than those of the similar federal program. No matter what resolution solution works for your situation, you may benefit from finding a tax professional well-versed in your state's tax system.

Most states offer a taxpayer advocate to assist with working out state tax issues. Again, the services provided will vary from state to state. Some states' tax advocates can help you resolve your debts from start to finish, although other states' advocates are there to help only if you feel you are being unfairly treated or harassed. Find out the extent of services your state provides.

Depending on your state's laws and practices, you may benefit from consumer credit counseling. Although most people know these organizations can help in dealing with credit card and other consumer debts, many are unaware that they may be able to help with tax debts as well. Be cautious in choosing an agency. Generally, you want to find a not-for-profit organization that is well rated by the Better Business Bureau and that has good rapport with your state tax board. Make sure you fully understand exactly what services they are providing for you before you sign any agreements or pay any fees.

A Word About Amnesty

Amnesty programs are gaining popularity in the tax world. During these amnesty periods, states agree to reduce or eliminate penalties, fines, and even criminal charges to those taxpayers who come forward and pay their debts in full. This can create a flush of much needed cash for the state, but some pundits believe these programs only result in more people hiding from the taxman and encourage people to shirk their tax obligations, knowing they can avoid the penalties during an amnesty program.

For better or worse, many people who are not experiencing active collection efforts will often stay in hiding from the government for fear of having to pay hefty penalties and fines. And many states use the funds—which, frankly, they didn't have access to anyway—to pay for stalled projects or just as an economic boost to get them through a budget shortfall.

As to the actual results of enforced collections vs. amnesty programs, that's up for debate. Starting in 2004, Nebraska has been offering annual tax amnesty programs. In 2009, the state collected $4.6 million through its tax amnesty program—certainly not chump change!

Fun State Tax Fast Facts

Least taxed state—Alaska: 6.4 percent of income. Alaska's state/local tax burden is well below the national average of 9.7 percent. (*Source*: Tax Foundation)

Most taxed state—New Jersey: Estimated at 11.8 percent of income, New Jersey's state/local tax burden percentage is the highest in the country, well above the national average of 9.7 percent. (*Source*: Tax Foundation)

10 percent—The average amount of state and local taxes taken out of your paycheck.

Best state to win the lottery in—Rhode Island, at 22 cents tax on each dollar won.

Worst state to be a winner—West Virginia, at 61 cents on each dollar.

Best state to live in if you have a bad smoking habit—South Carolina. You'll pay seven cents per pack compared to $1.19 in most other states. Don't forget the federal tax rate for cigarettes went up to more than $1 per pack in 2009. There's yet another reason to quit.

Worst place to live if you love the liquor—Oregon. The tax rate for the strong stuff is almost $21 per gallon compared to $1.50 per gallon in the nation's capital of Washington, D.C.

Vacation bound—Many states are increasing the taxes on rental cars and hotel rooms. See a pattern here? Items that are considered either luxuries or sins are being taxed more; that's why they call it a sin tax. I think the politicians figure if you can afford to have fun, you can afford to pay more taxes to do it!

States with no sales tax—The only states that don't collect sales tax are Alaska, Delaware, Montana, New Hampshire, and Oregon. (*Source*: Tax Foundation)

Some State "Tax Bailout" Options

Although every state is different, most are willing to work with you if you are having trouble paying your state taxes. Here are some examples of how some states work with taxpayers to resolve their tax debts.

CALIFORNIA

California uses an "Individual Electronic Installment Agreement." You can even apply online and then check the status of your application without leaving the house.

To make your application process go smoothly, be sure you have the following information ready to fill in: last name, Social Security number, bank account and routing numbers, and the total amount of state tax you owe. If you qualify for this streamlined repayment program, you will receive written notice within thirty days.

Generally, if you owe $10,000 or less and can commit to paying off the agreement in three years or less, you should be able to qualify for this installment plan. You must have filed all of your personal income tax returns as required. You must also commit to making the payments through an electronic funds transfer—which is why the state needs your banking information—and those payments are made on the state's schedule, not yours.

Like the federal Installment Agreement, your monthly payments are based on what you can afford to pay each month and are set at a minimum of $25 per month. You are also required to file all your future tax returns on time and pay any future tax balances by the assigned due date—meaning the Installment Agreement cannot become a revolving door for someone who racks up a debt every single year.

There is a nominal fee of $20 to set up the agreement but, all in all, it's a reasonable way to get caught up on your tax liability if you can't pay the entire bill all at once.

So, what if you owe more than $10,000? There is still hope for you. Remember, any tax agency, whether it's federal or state, has one main goal—to collect taxes, especially back taxes with all those penalties and interest charges attached. You may still be able to get an Installment Agreement, but you'll have to contact the California Franchise Tax Board directly to speak with someone who can help you work out a payment plan instead of using the state's online system.

California was so committed to helping its residents pay their back taxes that in past years, the Franchise Tax Board enacted two programs aimed at recovering delinquent tax debt. A Tax Amnesty program was established so taxpayers could settle their debt without fear of more dire consequences. Another program called the Voluntary Compliance Initiative focused on recouping taxes owed from people who used illegal tax shelters to avoid paying their fair share. Although those programs ended a few years back, I'm willing to bet we see more programs like these coming down the pike.

ARIZONA

In Arizona, Installment Agreements are offered and can be negotiated depending on your particular financial situation. You can even use your credit card to make payments, although I don't recommend that because you will be paying interest on the credit card debt. But if you have a card with an incredibly low interest rate or you have the ability to pay off your monthly balance in full, then by all means, go for it! It sure beats having the Arizona Department of Revenue hounding you for payment.

Arizona also has been known to waive penalties, negotiate a reduction of the outstanding debt, or grant temporary hardship considerations. Each of these possibilities can be negotiated by contacting the Arizona Department of Revenue directly.

ARKANSAS

Arkansas has an Offer in Compromise program through its Revenue Division of the Department of Finance and Administration. This is certainly not a tax debt free-for-all. You will have to qualify and show that you are suffering from an overwhelming tax debt. You will also have to pay a reasonable amount of the tax debt.

To apply for an Arkansas OIC, you will have to fill out an application, provide a bevy of financial documentation, and be ready to make the OIC payment upon acceptance.

Little Rhodie, Big Tax Tip

Here are a few tax tidbits from Rhode Island:

- You may now have to pay sales tax (7 percent) for online purchases. This is similar to New York's Amazon law, wherein any online retailer that also has a physical connection in the state will have to charge you sales tax, just like local shops.
- If you owe money to the state's medical assistance program, you can now have your personal income tax refund applied to reduce or completely offset the debt.
- Cancellation-of-debt income for businesses will now be taxed in the same year it is earned.
- As of January 1, 2010, Rhode Island eliminated the favorable tax treatment of capital gains. Now those investments will be taxed at ordinary income rates. Instead of paying 1.67 percent, these funds will be taxed at up to 9.9 percent.

The State Tax Man Cometh

In general, states rely on the same types of taxes to collect revenue from their citizens. I bet you're already familiar with most of these:

- Sales tax
- Income tax
- Property tax
- Estate and inheritance tax
- Fuel tax
- Licensing tax
- Retirement income tax
- State tax
- City tax
- Local or municipal tax

Many states charge a single rate throughout the state, although others also charge city, county, and local municipal taxes. States that charge single rates include: Connecticut, Hawaii, Indiana, Kentucky, Minnesota, Maryland, Massachusetts, Michigan, Mississippi, New Jersey, Rhode Island, Vermont, Virginia, and West Virginia.

Tale of the Tape

Check out this list to see if your state has raised taxes or expects to do so:

States that enacted new tax measures:

Arkansas, California, Colorado, Florida, Hawaii, Idaho, Iowa, Kansas, Kentucky, Maine, Maryland, Mississippi, Montana, Nevada, New York, Rhode Island, South Dakota, Utah, Vermont, Virginia, Washington, Wisconsin, Wyoming.

Source: CNN Money

States proposing new tax measures:

Arizona, Connecticut, Delaware, Illinois, Massachusetts, Michigan, New Hampshire, New Jersey, North Carolina, Ohio, Oregon, Pennsylvania, Tennessee.

The states with the highest local and state incomes taxes? New Jersey takes the cake and 11.8 percent of your money, followed by New York at 11.7 percent. Two of the most beautiful places you could live in the United States will also cost you—Hawaii at 10.6 percent and California at 10.5 percent. Other states in the top ten:

Connecticut—11.1 percent
Maryland—10.8 percent
Ohio—10.4 percent
Vermont—10.3 percent
Wisconsin—10.2 percent
Rhode Island—10.2 percent

State Income Tax

Some states do not charge income tax; although that may sound great in theory, remember, they are likely getting their revenue from you in other ways, like higher sales taxes or ridiculous property taxes. So before you move or retire to Florida or Nevada, you may want to consider your own personal situation.

States with No Income Tax:

Alaska, Florida, Nevada, South Dakota, Texas, Washington, and Wyoming.

State Sales Tax

Almost all states charge some form of sales tax, at least on certain goods and services. The only states that do not are Alaska, Delaware, Montana, New Hampshire, and Oregon.

Local/Municipal Tax Amnesty

A Tax Amnesty program intends to provide tax relief. Typically, an amnesty has a very short window of opportunity. The goal is to collect as much back tax as possible in a very short period of time, usually two or three months. Generally, the state will waive penalties if you file returns and pay your taxes during the amnesty period. And usually the state will impose larger than normal penalties if you fail to take action during the amnesty period. California, Michigan, and Ohio allow their municipalities to offer tax amnesties.

Philadelphia Mayor Michael Nutter has signed an ordinance that was passed by the city council in December 2009 providing a tax amnesty period that will occur over forty-five days in May and June 2010 and overlap with the state amnesty program. Under the terms of the amnesty bill, 100 percent of accrued penalties and 50 percent of accrued interest due on delinquencies are waived after the taxpayer makes all required payments.

Sounds too good to be true? Remember, the goal of the program is to collect as much of the tax delinquency as possible from an individual. Although penalties and interest may be waived, remember that you will still be responsible for the entire principal balance.

Property Taxes

Property taxes account for the largest portion of revenue for most states. Cities with the largest populations of high wage earners usually have the highest property tax rates. Unfortunately, property taxes often harm homeowners with low wages and the elderly disproportionately. Luckily, there are solutions. Because property taxes are set by the state or local government, there is no uniform method for requesting help with property taxes you cannot afford. Check with your state or local property tax board to see what relief they offer.

What kind of break might you expect? It really depends on where you live. All fifty states offer some type of property tax relief program, such as property tax freezes that lock in the assessed value of your property for homeowners over a certain age. Another option is a property tax deferral, through which the state pays your property taxes until you pass away or sell your home. Then it collects the property taxes, plus interest of course, from the sale proceeds. Many states also offer a homestead exemption, which exempts a certain amount of your property's value from taxes.

Your best bet is to contact your state's revenue department and ask it what options apply to you and your specific situation.

Save Money by Getting Your Home Reassessed

In an economic environment where property values in many states have hit rock bottom, one good way to save on taxes is to have your property reassessed. In most regions of the country, homes are worth 30–40 percent less than they were in 2005 and 2006. But your tax bill may not reflect that decline in value.

How to square things with your home's tax value? With a tax reassessment. Contact your county tax assessor's office and find out how to have your property taxes reassessed. To help your case, here are a few tips:

- Know the current market value of your home—this can be determined by speaking with a licensed Realtor®.
- Ask a Realtor for a list of recent comparable sales in your area that support your home's current market value.

This information will help convince the assessor that your home's value has changed, and thus your property taxes should be reduced.

Inheritance Tax

We've already talked about the federal estate tax, but some states collect their own share of an estate through two different taxes. Estate taxes are applied to an entire estate before it is distributed. Some states have an inheritance tax, which taxes the portion an individual beneficiary receives.

Although the federal estate tax still sits in limbo at the time of this writing, many states are still levying estate and inheritance taxes, according to their own state tax laws.

Currently, nineteen states and the District of Columbia tax inheritances and/or estates, many of them with no exemption limits. Some states limit the amount of the tax based on how closely related a person is to the decedent. As you can imagine, the rules are rather hairy. Taxpayers living in New Jersey and Maryland should take special note: these two states charge *both* estate and inheritance taxes. Talk about double dipping!

Kings of the Road

Truckers and tax professionals can have an eighteen-wheeler-sized headache in dealing with back taxes. One of the major reasons truckers get in trouble is the fact that they are expected to pay income taxes in every state in which they are licensed to drive.

For long-haul drivers, this adds up to a tax nightmare. Just figuring out what income was earned in which state is daunting enough, but when you tack on the registration fees, road usage fees, and any other taxes charged by each state, it's downright horrifying.

Federal Tax Debt Trumps State Tax Debt

If you have an outstanding federal tax debt, you should be aware of its implications for you at the state tax level. First, there is the State

Income Tax Levy Program. In this program, the IRS matches state income tax refunds with delinquent federal tax accounts. In finding a match, the state tax refunds may be levied by the IRS to satisfy an outstanding federal tax liability. This is for both individuals and businesses. So before you make plans for your expected state tax refund, better make sure the IRS doesn't have its grubby mitts on it.

Second, the IRS is not required to honor an existing state tax debt resolution program for purposes of determining whether to accept a proposed IRS tax debt resolution. For example, if you have a monthly payment in place to your state taxing authority, the IRS can disallow it as an expense and claim that the payment should be coming to it instead. Their reasoning—federal law (and tax obligations) preempts state law (and tax obligations). The IRS commonly disallows state tax installment agreements when considering proposed OICs.

This Is Your Tax Money on Drugs

By far, the most outrageous tax I can think of is a tax on something that is illegal. But more than ten states, from freewheeling Nevada to North Carolina and Alabama, expect you to pay taxes on the illegal drugs or moonshine in your possession. Of course, minimum quantities do apply. As of July 21, 2009, Oakland, California, became the first U.S. city to tax proceeds on medical marijuana. The law imposes

---

Health Crisis

Because you are already allowed to deduct medical expenses from your federal taxes, most states do not allow you to "double up" and deduct them from your state income taxes as well.

There are two exceptions: North Dakota and Oregon. These two states allow you to deduct fully your medical expenses on both your state and federal tax return.

Strange But True State Taxes

By this point in the book, you are probably beginning to wonder if there is anything that isn't taxed. Well, it's funny you should ask. Just for fun, here are some of the strangest taxes we've come across. They are definitely good for a laugh.

- **Baby, It's Cold Outside**—If you live in Minnesota, you'll have to pay extra to keep warm if you buy a fur coat. Other types of clothing are exempt from sales tax but not fur—that's taxable in the Land of a Thousand Lakes.
- **Hello, Sports Fans**—Many states, including Virginia, Maryland, and Massachusetts, charge an amusement tax if you buy tickets to any venue with more than 750 seats. So whether it's a Red Sox game or a Rolling Stones concert, the taxman will be joining you.
- **Jock Itch**—Okay, well, maybe not an itch, but some states and cities are itching to get extra money out of professional athletes and entertainers. Almost every state with a pro sports team charges the visiting team a tax on income earned while playing in their state. Talk about bad sportsmanship!
- **For Here or To Go?**—In Chicago, if you opt to drink soda, or pop as they call it, from a glass or cup, you'll pay a 9 percent tax. But take that drink with you in either a can or bottle and you pay just 3 percent. It pays to be mobile.
- **Fireworks Anyone?**—The state of West Virginia charges a special tax to anyone selling novelties and sparklers. I guess it's more expensive to be patriotic in West Virginia.
- **Sex Sells**—And it also gets taxed. If you own a business that deals in sexually explicit fun (e.g., nude dancers) in the state of Utah, you will pay 10 percent sales and use tax on things like the price of admission, drinks, and food.
- **Cry the Blues**—Believe it or not, if you deal in blueberries in the state of Maine, you are subject to an additional three-quarter-cent-per-pound tax.

a 1.8 percent gross receipts tax on the four licensed medical canna-
bis dispensaries in Oakland. These facilities would have to pay about
$18 in taxes for every $1,000 in marijuana sales. North Carolina will
even make it easy on you by providing you with stamps to prove
that you paid your taxes on your little bag of fun. The stamps are
courtesy of the Department of Revenue. When you walk in to pay
your taxes, revenue collectors are not allowed to ask for ID. Oddly
enough, not many folks have come forward to pay taxes on their illegal substances. Where the state really makes its money is when folks
get busted and their weed or moonshine doesn't have the stamp on
it. So far they've collected more than $78 million in illegal substance
taxes, not to mention a lot of baggies of pot! (Source: CCH, Inc., and
Tax Foundation)

Roni's Words of Wisdom

If you think that state governments will go softer on you than the
federal government should you fall behind on taxes, think again.

With unfunded mandates, lower tax revenues, pensions, and an
inflated, unchecked history of spending, states continue to hit up
taxpayers to close the gap on their fiscal deficits.

So if you receive a packet in the mail from your state's tax board,
don't sit on it and don't delay in doing two things:

1. Contact your state's tax office and let it know you are aware
   of the problem and are committed to addressing it.
2. Develop a plan—with or without a tax professional's guid-
   ance—to fix the problem. If you can pay, then pay. If you can
   agree to an Installment Agreement, then go that route. But if
   you owe a lot of money and need to start negotiating, I'd advise
   getting a reputable tax professional to watch your back.

The important thing is to move forward on your state tax debt.
Because, believe me on this one, your state won't ignore it.

−1

Washington Watch: What We Can Expect from Congress

Worried about an IRS audit? Avoid what's called a red flag. That's something the IRS always looks for. For example, say you have some money left in your bank account after paying taxes. That's a red flag.

—Jay Leno

Did you think that the fallout from the Great Recession would stop our elected representatives from feeding at the public trough?

You should know better. In fact, our elected officials' abuse of the public treasury has gone well beyond feeding from the trough and landed squarely in the realm of unchecked gluttony.

A recent report from the *Wall Street Journal* says the amount of money U.S. senators and members of the House of Representatives use on their own behalf has increased drastically over the past fifteen years. The findings have many Americans concerned, wondering why Congress is spending so much taxpayer money while the rest of the country is struggling to make ends meet.

According to the *Journal's* review of 60,000 travel documents, Congressional spending on overseas travel was up almost tenfold between 1995 and 2009 and has nearly tripled since 2001 alone. In 2008, at the vortex of the "worst financial crisis since the Great Depression," hundreds of lawmakers traveled overseas at a total cost of about $13 million to John Q. Public.

I don't mean to pick on Congress, even though it's a big, fat, juicy target.

The point is, remember, the same Congress that so boldly dips into the public trust by taking lavish trips during a time of economic calamity—and at a time when most American families can't even begin to think about vacation plans—is also the biggest influence on tax policy and fiscal responsibility.

Fiscal responsibility is clearly not our federal government's strong suit. Consider 2009, the first year of a new administration in the White House. Upon taking office, President Barack Obama and Congress passed a massive ($787 billion) stimulus bill, the American Recovery and Reinvestment Act of 2009 (2009 Recovery Act). Included in this legislation was a host of tax law changes that were supposed to buoy taxpayers, stimulate the economy, and jump start consumer spending. Here are just a few:

- New Making Work Pay credit
- Extended and expanded homebuyer credit
- New deduction for state and local sales taxes for purchases of motor vehicles
- Enhanced child tax credit
- COBRA premium assistance
- Enhanced transportation fringe benefits
- Increased energy tax breaks
- Extended net operating loss carryback for small businesses

Certainly, these tax breaks put a little more money in most American pockets. Great, right? Well, before we start giving out high fives, take a step back. At a time when our tax revenues are lower than ever, our deficit is higher than ever, and our economy continues to stall, we need to ask if these tax cuts will actually help us in the long run.

You see, these tax changes are a double-edged sword. Certainly, we all like tax breaks, and we should take advantage of every deduction and credit we've got coming. However, all these cuts are only perpetuating our country's economic problems. Increasing spending while cutting tax revenues just delays our fiscal woes for a few years, and in time we are going to have to pay for these tax breaks. How? Why, with more taxes, of course.

Coming Soon: More Taxes

Congress has been busy. Over the last year, it has been putting together some enormous pieces of legislation that will have enormous impact on us all.

Consider health care reform. President Obama signed the Patient Protection and Affordable Care Act into law on March 23, 2010. The $940 billion overhaul subsidizes coverage for uninsured Americans, financed by Medicare cuts to hospitals and fees or taxes on insurers, drug makers, medical-device companies, and Americans earning more than $200,000 a year. Many of the changes in the bill of more than 2,400 pages, such as requiring most people to have health insurance and employers to provide coverage, will take at least two years to go into effect.

Of course, health care for all is a wonderful idea. However, considering the pending tide of the coming tax disaster, I am definitely concerned about the increased role of the IRS through this reform package.

What we know is that the IRS has been delegated the task of "enforcing" the new health care law. And trust me, enforcing is not too strong of a word here, and this is why: Republicans on the House Ways and Means Committee warn that as many as 16,500 new IRS

Tax Implications of Proposed Health Care Bill

- 40 percent excise tax on "Cadillac" health coverage (in excess of $8,500 for individuals, $23,000 for families)
- Employer W-2 reporting of the value of health benefits (Note: this just forces your employer to report the value of your benefits. But watch out for these benefits to become taxable in the next few years.)
- Increase the penalty for nonqualified health savings account distributions to 20 percent
- Limit health flexible spending arrangements in cafeteria plans to $2,500
- $2.3 billion annual fee on manufacturers and importers of branded drugs
- Impose annual fee on manufacturers and importers of certain medical devices
- Impose annual fee on health insurance providers
- Eliminate deduction for expenses allocable to Medicare Part D subsidy
- Raise 7.5 percent AGI floor on medical expenses deduction to 10 percent (AGI floor for individuals age sixty-five and older remains at 7.5 percent through 2016)
- Raise the hospital insurance tax on wages and self-employment income in excess of $200,000 ($250,000 joint) by 0.9 percentage points
- 10 percent excise tax on indoor tanning services to take effect July 1, 2010

employees could be needed to enforce the new law at a cost of billions of dollars over the next ten years. This means we taxpayers will see more audits, confiscated refunds, and tax penalties masquerading as non-compliance fines. This does not sit well with me.

Bailouts Could Cost the United States $23 Trillion

According to an estimate from Politico.com, the federal bailouts from the recession years could end up costing a staggering $23 trillion. Although Neil Barofsky, the head of the federal bailout program and author of the government report that came up with the number, admits that this number is a "worst-case scenario," the government had only spent $2 trillion through mid-2009.

As a point of reference, the $23 trillion is more than the total combined cost of all the wars the United States has ever fought. World War II, for example, cost $4.1 trillion in 2008 dollars, according to the Congressional Research Service.

Even in today's dollars, the moon landings and the New Deal didn't come close to $23 trillion: the moon shot in 1969 cost an estimated $237 billion in current dollars, and the entire Depression-era Roosevelt relief program came in at $500 billion.

In comparison, the annual gross domestic product of the United States is just over $14 trillion.

Watch Out for New Taxes

To make up the gap between what the government needs and what the government collects in taxes, Washington will be busy over the next few years devising new ways to separate you from the money in your wallet. Keep an eye out for these new taxes (any of which could already be in place by the time you reach this page in the book!):

- **Letting the Bush Tax Cuts Expire**—President Obama's 2011 budget calls for letting the top two tax brackets go up to 36 and 39.6 percent respectively.
- **Reduction in Tax Breaks for Large Corporations**—This would stop corporations with foreign income from claiming deductions against their foreign income, until the income is reported to the IRS (currently, foreign income can be deferred, while deductions are still taken).
- **Tax on Stocks**—The "Let Wall Street Pay for the Restoration of Main Street Act of 2009" proposed a 0.25 percent tax on purchasing securities.
- **Value-Added Tax**—A tax levied on manufacturers at each stage of production on the amount of value the producer adds to the product. Although there is no specific proposal before Congress regarding the value-added tax, in a recent interview, President Obama stated that the value-added tax has worked for other countries and "would be novel for the United States."
- **War Tax**—The "Share the Sacrifice Act" creates a graduated surtax on anyone with taxable income, from 1 percent for the lowest income levels up to 5 percent for the highest-earning households.

How Tax Increases Could Impact the Wealthy

America's wealthy already pay most of our state and federal taxes. But that doesn't mean much to Uncle Sam. There's more bloodletting on the horizon if the White House and Congress get their way. According to the Heritage Foundation, potential tax increases to shore up the government's spending gap could really sock it to the wealthy. Here is what the well-off may see in future tax hikes:

- A family of four making $450,000 a year would pay $103,600 in federal income taxes, an increase of $1,000.

- A single filer making $450,000 a year would pay $112,200 in federal income taxes, an increase of $7,100.
- A family of four making $800,000 a year would pay $220,800 in federal income taxes, an increase of $30,000.
- A single filer making $800,000 a year would pay $231,300 in federal income taxes, an increase of $30,700.
- A family of four making $5 million a year would pay $1.81 million in federal income taxes, an increase of $443,500.
- A single filer making $5 million a year would pay $1.83 million in federal income taxes, an increase of $452,000.

Taxing Complexity

You can't swing a crooked lobbyist without hitting someone who thinks the current tax system is too complicated.

Yet with near-universal agreement on that sentiment, our elected representatives keep making the tax code even *more* complicated.

But there's a legitimate school of thought that states the government abhors simplicity. It's a much better strategy for politicians to confuse Americans with the tax code, making it easier to raise more revenue through a confusing taxation system.

Think about it. The political process, almost by definition, creates confusion. Creatures of Washington—meaning Congress, lobbyists, lawyers, and other special interest groups—love those targeted tax breaks and subsidies. The problem is that specific tax subsidies wind up complicating the tax system by building layers and layers of new statutes in the tax code.

Let's look at the facts:

- Income taxes are so complex that IRS Commissioner Doug Shulman recently admitted he does not prepare his own taxes. If the head of the IRS can't figure out his tax obligations, how are we all supposed to?

- As the income tax system grows more complex, the number of IRS tax forms has jumped from 402 in 1990 to more than 900 by 2008.

- Congress promotes discrimination through the tax code. The front of the Supreme Court building boldly declares "equal justice under law," yet the income tax has hundreds of discriminatory provisions. For example, homeowners are treated more favorably than renters because they can deduct mortgage interest and other itemized deductions. Consider that a higher-income homeowner can effectively deduct car loan interest by shifting around his finances but a lower-income apartment dweller cannot.

- Congress frequently holds hearings on tax simplification so members can denounce the tax code's complexity. Each time, Congressional experts and outside think tanks provide useful simplification ideas. Then, when the TV cameras are turned off, Congress promptly ignores them and votes for more special interest breaks. The result: the number of pages in the tax code and regulations nearly tripled from 26,300 in 1984 to more than 70,000 by 2008.

- For years, officials have hailed the income tax as "our voluntary tax system." The IRS says that it pursues "enforcement programs to promote voluntary compliance" and establishes "strategies to maximize voluntary tax law compliance by emphasizing customer satisfaction." But with thirty-two million IRS penalties assessed each year and about $10,000 in income taxes imposed on each tax-paying household, the tax isn't voluntary and these customers aren't satisfied.

- Although the income tax is ninety-seven years old, Congress still can't figure out what exactly is meant by "income." Some income, such as municipal bond interest, is not taxed, but other income, such as dividends, is taxed twice. The income tax treatment of savings is particularly incoherent and unstable. For example, there have been twenty-five major changes in the capital gains tax since 1922.

- Shouldn't saving for education, retirement, and other items be as simple as putting money in the bank? Instead, Congress has manufactured hundreds of special savings rules, such as 401(k)s, Keoghs, deductible IRAs, nondeductible IRAs, education IRAs, Roth IRAs, traditional pension plans, annuities, SIMPLEs, SEPs, MSAs, and others. The IRS guide to IRAs alone is 105 pages long.

Roni's Words of Wisdom

What's the best way to rein in the IRS and create a simpler, fairer tax code that works for everyone? I've got a few ideas. So pay attention, Washington—it's time to hit the reset button on taxes and start from scratch:

- **Get rid of the AMT:** In a case of good intentions gone awry, the alternative minimum tax was created to ensure that high-income taxpayers pay at least some income tax. Unfortunately, the law was written so poorly that it now affects as many as four million taxpayers, mostly people who already pay significant amounts of income tax and are far from the top of the income scale. Rather than having to "patch" the AMT year after year, get rid of the darn thing, once and for all.

- **Simplify the tax code:** Get rid of an overly complex, overly progressive system of taxation. In 2008, the Internal Revenue Service estimated the average taxpayer lost 26.4 hours to preparing a tax return, up to 56.9 hours if a Schedule C for business or a Schedule E for rental properties was filed. That's way too long—simplify the tax code and give Americans their lives back every April.

- **Stop taxing Social Security and other government benefits:** Taxing government benefits, like Social Security and unemployment income, is just plain ridiculous. Taxpayers all pay into these systems, then when they receive benefits from their years of pitching in, they then have to pay taxes on those, too? And usually when people are collecting these benefits they can least afford to lose a portion of the funds to taxes.

- **Stop double taxing certain forms of income:** Politicians love to target capital gains, interest, and dividends—it's a chance to dig into the pockets of those "fat cats" who have so much disposable income. Here's the problem: about half of all Americans have some form of investment, so these taxes hardly apply to only the wealthy. Look, we already paid taxes on the income when we earned it, now we have to pay taxes on it again? Not only is that just plain irksome, it's also unbelievably confusing between figuring out holding periods, what exactly constitutes a dividend, and how the taxes are paid on them. Let's scrap the whole deal and save investors and taxpayers the trouble.

- **Consolidate tax-favored retirement savings:** Americans have no shortage of ways to save for retirement, including deductible, nondeductible, and Roth IRAs, regular and Roth 401(k)s and similar plans, as well as traditional employment-based pension plans. But honestly, it seems to me that in this case, variety is working against us. The tax rules for each of these savings plans are complex and unnecessarily restrictive. Better to create one type of "super" plan with the same restrictions and tax rules. This would reduce taxpayer confusion and save us all from a mountain of paperwork come tax time.

- **Consolidate programs benefiting households with children:** Our government loves to help out families with children. Between Child Tax Credits, Dependent Care Credits, the Earned Income Tax Credit, and more, how are we supposed to make sense of it all? Instead of making taxpayers complete multiple worksheets to see what credits and deductions their children make them eligible for, let's consolidate and simplify the process with one overarching credit, with simple eligibility requirements.

12

Final Tips and Resources

Did you ever notice that when you put the words "The" and "IRS" together, it spells "THEIRS?"

—Author Unknown

I f there's one thing I've learned in all the years that I've gone to bat for taxpayers needing a bailout from the IRS, it's this: a little education goes a long way.

I remember an episode of *The Tonight Show*, where *South Park* creators Matt Stone and Trey Parker sat on the couch with Jay Leno. "So how did you guys meet?" Leno asked. "Actually," Stone replied, "we met in college." Leno's next question? "Whoa, you guys went to college!?"

Good joke, but who's laughing now? With an offbeat education on the foibles of U.S. culture, Stone and Parker turned a cartoon about four foul-mouthed but street-savvy little kids into a huge financial windfall.

Hey, tax education can pay off big time, too. That's why I want to end the book with loads of good resources to help you get—and stay—ahead of your tax troubles.

Call me an optimist, but I believe these Roni-tested, Roni-approved tax tips can help you get your share of the tax bailout, or at least the portion you deserve and may not know about.

Save Your Home from the IRS

Fight the tax lien—the odds might seem like they're against you, but you have more options than you think. Take these tips into consideration when battling a tax lien against your home:

- **Note the "five-day" rule.** By law, the IRS must notify you in writing within five business days after it files a tax lien.
- **Know your rights.** You are entitled to ask an IRS manager to review your case and you may request a Collection Due Process hearing with the Office of Appeals by filing with the office listed on your notice, but you must file this by the date listed on your notice.
- **Know the statute of limitations.** There is a statute of limitations that sets a timeframe in which the IRS has to collect the tax. If that expires before the IRS files the tax lien, you may be able to get the lien removed.
- **Pay off a lien through an Offer in Compromise.** Do you have some cash to pay off part of a lien but not the whole thing? The IRS may allow you to settle your debt through a reduced lump sum payment. The program is known as an Offer in Compromise (OIC). For more information on the OIC program, see chapter 9.
- **Pay off a lien through an Installment Agreement.** If you have enough wiggle room in your budget, you may be able to negotiate an Installment Agreement (IA), which will allow

you to pay back all or part of your tax liability to the IRS in monthly payments.

- **Wait it out.** It's not likely—but it's not impossible. Yes, your debt may expire before more serious action is taken. Note this option can be dangerous, as the IRS will often find reasons to extend the statute of limitations on a tax liability. Talk to a tax specialist before you play the waiting game.

Job and Employment Issues

With unemployment at historically high rates, knowing your tax rights on the job—and after you've been laid off—can mean the difference between a world of plenty and a world of hurt.

- **Protect your 401(k) from taxes.** Some 401(k) retirement plans let you leave your money invested when you leave your job. To protect your 401(k) money, ask your former employer to deposit it directly into a rollover account you set up for the transfer. That lets you avoid having 20 percent withheld for income taxes. No tax is due if you roll the money over, but withholding is automatic if you take possession of the funds.

- **Laid off? Call the IRS.** If you already have an arrangement with the IRS, such as an OIC or IA, and you get laid off, contact the IRS right away. That's getting ahead of the problem and can help you negotiate a more reasonable deal with the IRS. You may even be placed into a protected status, like Currently Not Collectible (CNC), until you have a consistent stream of income.

- **Watch out for unemployment taxes.** If you've received unemployment benefits, make sure you get Form 1099-G, reflecting total unemployment compensation for the year. Enter the amount on line nineteen of Form 1040.

- **If you're looking for work, take your tax deductions.** Log all job-search-related fees and expenses, including miles driven, employment agency fees, supplies, mailing expenses, phone calls, Internet job site fees, and career-related coaching.

Protect Your Small Business from the IRS

As a small business owner, I can tell you straight up: watch your wallet. Keep these tips in mind when dealing with taxes and your business:

- **Pay your self-employment tax.** If you are self-employed or a sole proprietor and collect 1099s at the end of the year, you must pay self-employment tax, whether you like it or not. Failure to do so will land you in a world of hurt. By paying your estimated taxes, including your self-employment taxes, on a quarterly basis you can avoid having to pay a larger chunk of money all at once.
- **Take the "Made in USA" tax break.** As of 2010, if more than 50 percent of your products are made in the United States, you are entitled to a federal tax deduction. The amount will equal 10 percent of your adjusted gross income or 10 percent of income received from those products sold. Check your state laws for similar tax breaks.
- **Go green, save green.** The government has gone green and it gives you tax incentives do to the same. For a complete list of green incentives, Google the phrase "Database for State Incentives for Renewables and Efficiency." Similarly, search EnergyStar.gov for qualifying appliances.
- **Take a business loan deduction.** If you take out a business loan, you can deduct the principal and interest that you pay on the loan. But if you negotiate to have your debt reduced

or forgiven, that amount becomes income and you will have to pay taxes on it.

- **Know state small business tax laws.** Any income that is made outside of your business's home state may not be taxable income. This only applies in half of all states so you will need to discuss the details with your tax professional.

- **Don't forget about business loss deductions.** Under Section 1244 of the IRS tax code, if you sell your company stock for a loss or you have to liquidate your business, you may be able to deduct the full amount from your income. There is a limit for this deduction; it maxes out at $50,000 or $100,000 if you are married and file jointly, and there are other conditions that apply, so consult your tax advisor about your specific situation.

- **Don't hide income.** The last thing you want to do if you are a small—or big—business owner is hide income or assets from Uncle Sam. Taking deductions that you are legally entitled to is one thing; falsifying your bookkeeping records to avoid paying taxes on a portion of your income—or *cooking the books* as it's termed—will not work out in your favor in the long run.

Tax Tips for Real-Life Problems

As John F. Kennedy once said, life is unfair. That goes double for life setbacks like divorce, illness, death in the family, bankruptcy, and other personal life crises. If one of these strikes you, take these measures to keep the IRS at bay:

- **Protect yourself in divorce.** Use the Innocent Spouse Relief stipulation that I explained in detail in chapter 7 (IRS Form 8857, Request for Innocent Spouse Relief) to guard your tax interest in a divorce. Know that the IRS is required by law to inform your ex or current spouse when you file for Innocent Spouse Relief. There are no exceptions, not even for victims of spousal abuse. But don't fret, your current address, employer, new name, and other personal information will not be disclosed.

- **Know about alimony taxes.** Alimony and child support are tricky items, particularly if you're not prepared for a divorce. Depending upon the terms of your divorce agreement, any alimony you pay may be deductible (even if you don't itemize), although alimony you receive may be taxable. What's more, alimony you receive is considered earned income for purposes of contributing to an IRA. Child support payments you make are not deductible, and any such payments you receive are not taxable.

- **Make sure your deductions, credits and exemptions are legitimate.** If you're hurting for money, the worst possible mistake you can make while filing a tax return is claiming a deduction for which you do not qualify. A lot of taxpayers make the mistake of assuming that they qualify for credits and exemptions when they don't. One good example of this is the child tax credit—although it seems like anyone with a kid should be eligible, there are a lot of qualifications of which you may not be aware. Always double- and triple-check any deductions, exemptions or credits.

- **Cover debt.** If you're struggling to stay afloat financially and are unable to pay your full tax bill by the due date, act fast to set up an alternative payment method. By calling the IRS or having a tax specialist do so, you can set up an Installment Agreement with the IRS, which will let you pay your debt off in monthly payments. This is a much better choice than tax evasion, which could result in hefty fines and penalties.

- **Seek out a hardship exemption.** If you already owe back taxes to the IRS and you suddenly become too ill to continue working, you may qualify to have your financial status adjusted. But you must contact either the tax specialist you are working with or the IRS directly to see if you qualify for a reduced payment plan, pay-off amount, or placement into CNC.

- **Bankruptcy does not mean a free ride.** If you've exhausted all of your options and must file for bankruptcy, don't assume that you will automatically be absolved of any back tax liability you owe the IRS. Chapter 7 and Chapter 13 are the only types of bankruptcy filing that allow you to discharge tax debt, and not all tax debts are dischargeable through bankruptcy.

- **'Til death do us part.** Although the death of a loved one (or even a not-so-beloved family member) is difficult to begin with, there will be a few final tax matters that must be cleared up before you can move on. A final tax return must be filed for a deceased person, and if the departed left behind a mountain of debt or a pile of assets and no will, you would be wise to hire an attorney who is experienced in settling estates as the probate process can be drawn out and complicated.

- **Inheritance money is not always free.** Although most money received through an inheritance is considered tax-free income, there are exceptions. Money that came from retirement accounts or annuities will be taxable to the receiver of that inheritance. Be aware of this rule and your specific state's rules when working on estate planning measures.

Protect Your Investment Income with These Tips

Wall Street has taken a beating the last few years, so it's vital to hang on to every nickel you can (after all, those nickels are hard to come by).

- **Take advantage of tax harvesting.** Tax harvesting is all about balancing investment losses with investment gains to your tax advantage. With tax harvesting, you can use your investment losses to soak up capital gains on a dollar-for-dollar basis. If your losses exceed your gains or you have no gains at all, you can deduct as much as $3,000 a year ($1,500 for those married and filing separately) of your net capital losses from your ordinary income. Excess amounts are carried over into future years. Remember, you actually have to sell securities and realize your losses in order for them to count.

- **Deduct your investment expenses.** Investment-wise, there is no shortage of deductions you can take off your taxes. See chapter 7 for a list of deductions you can take.
- **Hardship withdrawals**. The IRS, bless it, does allow hardship withdrawals from retirement accounts for serious economic problems, such as unemployment or an illness or injury. Just make sure you check with your plan administrator to see what hardship options are available to you. Be prepared to pay the 10 percent IRS penalty even if you're granted hardship status.
- **Be generous.** If you've made a windfall of profits in a particular year, instead of paying more money in taxes on that gain, why not consider donating some of your good fortune to your favorite charitable organization? You can also give money away tax-free if you pay for someone's medical or higher education expenses. And it feels good to pay it forward.

Tips for Negotiating with the IRS

At the heart of just about every deal we cut with the IRS are negotiations. The back and forth between tax specialists and the taxman can spell the difference between winning and losing your case with the government—and could mean tens or even hundreds of thousands of dollars coming out of your pocket. So take these tips on negotiating with the IRS and use them well:

- **Get current.** Prior to meeting with the IRS, make sure that you are current on all income tax filings.
- **Figure out the formula.** The IRS prefers to work off calculations to figure out how much you can afford to pay. To help calculate this figure, use Forms 656 and 433-A.
- **Form 433-A, B.** If your goal is to pay less than the full amount of taxes you owe, expect the IRS to request information about your finances via Form 433-A. Use Form 433-B if dealing with IRS tax debt for an organized business (e.g., corporation, etc.).
- **Communicate right now.** Once you hear that you're behind on your taxes (usually in a packet mailed "special delivery"), act fast. Specifically, don't put off calling or contacting the IRS about your back taxes. The more you procrastinate, the more it will cost you in interest and penalties on what you owe.
- **Contact a reputable tax specialist.** For the average taxpayer, trying to get through to the IRS can be a daunting task sometimes. To even the odds, get a tax specialist. A good tax pro knows the shortcuts, knows who to talk to, and knows what kind of deals can be cut. You'll have a tough time figuring that out on your own.
- **Try to work out a resolution.** If you can't score an Offer in Compromise, the IRS will sit down with you and work out payment arrangements to pay back what you owe it, plus interest and any penalties. Sometimes it does this via the mail and phone.
- **Protect yourself from state taxes.** Back tax problems can come at you from two sides: the federal government and

the often-overlooked state tax board. Make sure to educate yourself on both federal and state tax strategies.

- **Get your records in order.** So you have a state back tax problem? Then develop a plan, starting with the collection and organization of old tax records like W-2 and 1099 forms.

- **Watch out for property taxes.** Property taxes account for the largest portion of revenue for most states, and this includes personal property and business property tax. Stay on top of your property tax obligations and find out what property tax relief options are available in your state.

- **Watch out for the State Income Tax Levy Program (SITLP).** If your state income tax refund goes missing, thank the SITLP. If you have a delinquent federal tax debt, don't count on receiving your state tax refund.

- **Collect your tax forms**. To get blank state tax forms you might need to complete, visit your state's tax website. It should have information on how to download and print state tax forms, as well as information on how to file tax forms electronically. The website should also have accurate information on deadlines for back taxes and what the penalties and fees may be.

State Tax Departments and Websites

Many of the state websites also list several branch or district offices, so be sure to check out your state's site for more specific information. Also, several states have a taxpayer advocate who can assist you if you are having tax-related financial problems.

ALABAMA

Department of Revenue
50 North Ripley Street
Montgomery, AL 36132
334-242-1170
http://www.ador.state.al.us

ALASKA

Department of Revenue
Anchorage Office
550 W 7th Ave Ste. 500
Anchorage, AK 99501-3555
907-269-6620
http://www.tax.state.ak.us/

ARIZONA

Department of Revenue
Taxpayer Information &
   Assistance
PO Box 29086
Phoenix, AZ 85038-9086
602-255-3381
800-352-4090 (from 520 or 928
   area code)
http://www.revenue.state.az.us

ARKANSAS

Department of Finance and
   Administration
Revenue Division
1816 West Seventh Street,
   Room 2300
Ledbetter Building
Little Rock, AR 72201
501-682-7225
http://www.arkansas.gov/dfa/

CALIFORNIA

Franchise Tax Board
PO Box 942840
Sacramento, CA 94240-0040
916-464-1056 (interstate office)
800-689-4776
800-852-5711
Taxpayer Rights
   Advocate—800-883-5910
http://www.ftb.ca.gov

COLORADO

Department of Revenue
1375 Sherman
Denver, CO 80261-0009
303-534-1208 or 800-332-2085
http://www.revenue.state.co.us

CONNECTICUT

Department of Revenue
25 Sigourney Street Ste 2
Hartford, CT 06106-5032
860-297-5962
800-382-9463 (within state)
http://www.ct.gov/drs

DELAWARE

Department of Revenue
Carvel State Office Building
820 North French Street
Wilmington, DE 19801
302-577-8200
http://revenue.delaware.gov

DISTRICT OF COLUMBIA

Office of Tax and Revenue
941 North Capital Street NE 1st
 Floor
Washington, DC 20002
202-727-4829
http://otr.cfo.dc.gov/otr/site/
 default.asp

FLORIDA

Department of Revenue
General Tax Administration
5050 W Tennessee Street, D-1
Tallahassee, FL 32399-0100
800-352-3671
http://dor.myflorida.com/dor/

GEORGIA

Department of Revenue
Atlanta Headquarters
1800 Century Center Blvd., NE
Atlanta, GA 30345-3205
404-417-4480 (Metro Atlanta
 area)
877-602-8477
https://etax.dor.ga.gov

HAWAII

Department of Taxation
Oahu (Honolulu)
PO Box 259
Honolulu, HI 96809-0259
808-587-4242
800-222-3229
Taxpayer Advocate
808-587-1791
http://hawaii.gov/tax/

IDAHO

State Tax Commission
800 Park Blvd, Plaza IV
Boise, ID 83712
208-334-7660
800-972-7660
http://tax.idaho.gov

ILLINOIS

Department of Revenue
James R. Thompson Center
Concourse Level
100 West Randolph Street
Chicago, IL 60601-3274
312-814-5232
800-732-8866
http://www.revenue.state.il.us

INDIANA

Department of Revenue
100 N. Senate Avenue
Indianapolis, IN 46204
317-233-4018
http://www.in.gov/dor/index.
htm

IOWA

Department of Revenue
Hoover State Office Building
1305 E. Walnut
Des Moines, IA 50319
515-281-3114
800-367-3388
http://www.iowa.gov/tax/

KANSAS

Department of Revenue, Withholding Tax Unit
Robert B. Docking State Office
Building
Topeka, KS 66625-0001
913-296-0222
http://www.ink.org/public/kdor

KENTUCKY

Revenue Cabinet
Frankfort, KY 40620
502-564-7270 (also twelve
regional offices)
http://revenue.ky.gov/

LOUISIANA

Department of Revenue
PO Box 201
Baton Rouge, LA 70821-0201
225-925-4611
http://www.rev.state.la.us

MAINE

Maine Revenue Services Income
Tax Division
State Office Building
Augusta, ME 04333-0024
207-626-8475
http://www.state.me.us/revenue/

MARYLAND

Comptroller of the Treasury
Revenue Administration
  Division
Income Tax Building
Annapolis, MD 21411-0001
410-260-7980
http://www.marylandtaxes.com/

MASSACHUSETTS

Department of Revenue
100 Cambridge Street
PO Box 7022
Boston, MA 02204
617-727-4545
800-392-6089 (within MA)
http://www.dor.state.ma.us/

MICHIGAN

Income Tax Division
City-County Building
Detroit, MI 48226
313-224-3315
http://www.ci.detroit.mi.us

MINNESOTA

Department of Revenue
10 River Park Plaza
St. Paul, MN 55146
612-282-9999
800-657-3594
http://www.taxes.state.mn.us

MISSISSIPPI

State Tax Commission
PO Box 960
Jackson, MS 39205
601-359-1141
http://www.mstc.state.ms.us

MISSOURI

Department of Revenue
PO Box 3333
Jefferson City, MO 65105-3333
573-751-3683
http://dor.mo.gov/

MONTANA

Department of Revenue
PO Box 5835
Helena, MT 59604-5835
406-444-3388
http://discoveringmontana.com/
  revenue/css/default.asp

NEBRASKA

Department of Revenue
Nebraska State Office Building
301 Centennial Mall South
PO Box 94818
Lincoln, NE 68509-4818
402-471-5729
800-742-7474
http://www.revenue.state.ne.us/
  index.html

NEVADA

Department of Taxation
1550 College Parkway
Carson City, NV 89706
775-684-2000
http://tax.state.nv.us/

NEW HAMPSHIRE

Department of Revenue
    Administration
109 Pleasant Street
PO Box 457
Concord, NH 03302-0457
603-271-2191
Taxpayer Advocate
603-271-2191
http://www.revenue.nh.gov/con-
    tact/index.htm

NEW JERSEY

Division of Taxation
Gross Income Tax
CN 248
Trenton, NJ 08648-0248
609-588-2200
800-323-4400 (within NJ)
http://www.state.nj.us/treasury/
    taxation/

NEW MEXICO

Taxation and Revenue
    Department
PO Box 630
Santa Fe, NM 87509-0630
505-827-0700
http://www.state.nm.us/tax/

NEW YORK

Department of Taxation and
    Finance
Income Tax Bureau
W.A. Harriman Campus
Albany, NY 12227-0125
518-438-8581
800-225-5829 (within NY)
http://www.tax.state.ny.us/

NORTH CAROLINA

Department of Revenue
PO Box 25000
Raleigh, NC 27640
919-733-4626
http://www.dor.state.nc.us/

NORTH DAKOTA

State Tax Commissioner
State Capitol
600 E. Boulevard Avenue
Bismarck, ND 58505-0599
800-638-2901, Ext. 3124
701-328-3124
www.nd.gov/tax/

OHIO

Department of Taxation
PO Box 2476
Columbus, OH 43266-0076
614-846-6712
800-282-1780 (within OH)
http://tax.ohio.gov/

OKLAHOMA

Oklahoma Tax Commission
2501 Lincoln Boulevard
Oklahoma City, OK 73194
405-521-3155
http://www.oktax.state.ok.us

OREGON

Department of Revenue
Revenue Building
955 Center Street, NE
Salem, OR 97310
503-378-4988 or 945-8091
http://www.dor.state.or.us

PENNSYLVANIA

Department of Revenue
Department 280903
Harrisburg, PA 17128-0903
717-787-8201
http://www.revenue.state.pa.us

PUERTO RICO

Department of the Treasury
Bureau of Income Tax
Intendente Alejandro Ramirez
  Building
Paseo Covadonga, Stop 1
PO Box S-4515
San Juan, PR 00903
787-725-8835
http://www.hacienda.gobierno.
  pr

RHODE ISLAND

Division of Taxation
One Capitol Hill
Providence, RI 02908-5800
401-277-6400
http://www.tax.state.ri.us

SOUTH CAROLINA

Department of Revenue and
  Taxation
Box 125
Columbia, SC 29214
803-737-4752
http://www.sctax.org/default.
  htm

SOUTH DAKOTA

Department of Revenue &
  Regulation
445 East Capitol Avenue
Pierre, SD 57501
605-773-3311
http://www.state.sd.us/drr2/rev-
  enue.html

TENNESSEE

Department of Revenue
Andrew Jackson Building
500 Deaderick St.
Nashville, TN 37242
800-342-1003
615-253-0600 (Nashville and
  out-of-state)
http://www.state.tn.us/revenue/

TEXAS

Taxpayer Services and
  Collections
Central Services Building
1711 San Jacinto Blvd., Suite
  180
Austin, TX 78701-1416
512-463-4865
http://www.window.state.tx.us/
  taxes/

UTAH

State Tax Commission
210 North 1950 West
Salt Lake City, UT 84134
801-297-2200
800-662-4335 (within UT)
http://tax.utah.gov/index.html

VERMONT

Department of Taxes
PO Box 547
Montpelier, VT 05601-0547
802-828-2551
http://www.state.vt.us/tax/

VIRGINIA

Department of Taxation
Division of Income Tax
  Withholding
PO Box 1880
Richmond, VA 23282-1880
804-367-8037
http://www.tax.virginia.gov/

WASHINGTON

Department of Revenue
Taxpayer Rights Advocate
Taxpayer Services Division
PO Box 47478
Olympia, WA 98504-7478
800-647-7706
http://dor.wa.gov/Content/
  Home/Default.aspx

WEST VIRGINIA

State Tax Commissioner
Capitol Complex, Building 1,
  W417
Charleston, WV 25305
304-558-3333
800-982-8297
http://www.state.wv.us/taxdiv

WISCONSIN

Department of Revenue
PO Box 8910
Madison, WI 53708
608-266-2776
http://www.dor.state.wi.us/

WYOMING

Department of Revenue
Herschler Bldg, 2nd Floor West
Cheyenne, WY 82002-0110
307-777-7961
http://revenue.state.wy.us/

Now It's Up To You

Fighting back against tax problems and earning your own financial bailout isn't easy, but I hope that the book you hold in your hands gives you the courage, knowledge, and confidence to take the IRS on—head on.

As a tax professional who has fought—and won—against the IRS in thousands of cases, I know it can be done, and I know you can do it.

Now, the rest is up to you. As a wise man once said, the longest journey begins with a single step.

I hope, and I believe, that this book is your first step.

I also believe that this first step is the start of a rewarding, fulfilling, and profitable experience for you. After all, beating the IRS at its own game is high atop the list of most satisfying accomplishments anyone can ever have.

Now it's your turn to have the same feeling.

Acknowledgements

I want to acknowledge and thank the most amazing people I get to play with everyday at "school": Justin, Arica, Nicole, and Gretchen. Thank you for the joy you bring into my life. I hope you feel appreciated, respected, and loved. And by the way, hold on for the ride of your life!!!! I would also like to acknowledge and thank GOD for the many, many blessings in my life.

Coming in January, the 2011 edition
of Roni's first book,
"The Lady's Guide to Beating the IRS
and Saving Big Bucks on Your Taxes."
Order your copy now.

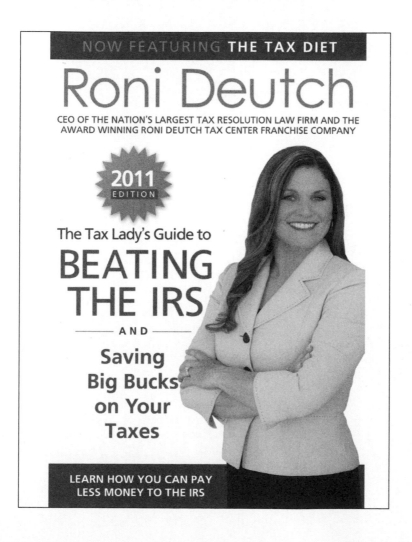